D0205369

The Antislavery Rank and File

Recent Titles in
Contributions in American History

The Antislavery Rank and File

A SOCIAL PROFILE OF THE ABOLITIONISTS' CONSTITUENCY

Edward Magdol

CONTRIBUTIONS IN AMERICAN HISTORY, NUMBER 117

GREENWOOD PRESS

NEW YORK
WESTPORT, CONNECTICUT
LONDON

Library of Congress Cataloging-in-Publication Data

Magdol, Edward.
   The antislavery rank and file.

   (Contributions in American history, ISSN 0084-9219 ;
no. 117)
   Bibliography: p.
   Includes index.
   1. Abolitionists—United States.   2. Slavery—
United States—Anti-slavery movements.   I. Title.
II. Series.
E449.M19   1986   326'.0973   85-30191
ISBN 0-313-24723-4

Library of Congress Catalog Card Number: 85-30191
ISBN: 0-313-24723-4
ISSN: 0084-9219

First published in 1986

Greenwood Press, Inc.
88 Post Road West
Westport, Connecticut 06881

Printed in the United States of America

The paper used in this book complies with the
Permanent Paper Standard issued by the National
Information Standards Organization (Z39.48-1984).

10 9 8 7 6 5 4 3 2 1

Contents

Tables

Note to the Reader

This work was very close to completion at the time of Edward Magdol's sudden death on October 6, 1984. His files and desk were overflowing with chapters, new and old, revised and in revision. Pages "to be typed" and new thoughts "to be included" were inserted here and there. Readers' comments were available and folders of tables, computer printouts and source material were most plentiful. Footnotes awaited reorganization.

Two of us, one his wife and sometime co-worker, the other a friend and colleague, joined together to prepare the manuscript for publication.

Minimal changes have been made, and these only when the notes so directed. Ed's final revisions were to include an expansion of Chapter 8 (see our note 18 in that chapter), the inclusion of additional anecdotal and biographical information about individual signers, and possibly additional background information on some of the New England cities (tasks we did not attempt).

The sources of a number of quotations had not yet been noted on the manuscript. We have been able to locate all but two of the references.

We hope that Ed would be satisfied with the final product.

If there are errors of judgment in the editing we must take full responsibility.

Miriam Sper Magdol
Michael A. Gordon

Data collected for this project are available on computer tape and can be obtained from the Inter-university Consortium for Political and Social Research, P.O. Box 1248, Ann Arbor, MI 48106, (313) 764-2570.

Preface

In a compelling article written in 1964, Betty Fladeland asked: "Who were the abolitionists?" Her answer destroyed myths and distortions about these radical reformers.[1] It also set the stage for further research and development of the question. Three years later David Brion Davis suggested that records of abolition societies and the petitions they generated could furnish evidence about the nature of the rank and file members of the abolitionist movement.[2] This book follows in the paths begun by Professors Fladeland and Davis. It relies in great measure upon analysis of abolitionist petitions.

The resulting social profile of the antislavery constituency helps us to appreciate the abolitionist crusade in a new light. It reflects the complex social relationships within which the movement grew. It also calls into question some conventional views about labor's attitudes toward the antislavery movement. Finally, it offers concrete new evidence of the movement's political complexion.

The identification of the antislavery rank and file is complicated by its environment of social, economic, and political change. A busy and restless crossroad in American history was marked by the intersection of the abolitionist movement with early industrialization in the Northeast, creation of an assertive, self-conscious, and ambitious middle class and its subordinate factory working class, an elastic polity being stretched to include more whites and to exclude blacks, and the re-entrenchment of slavery in the deep South. The first impulses of common sense suggested connections among these processes.

Further study rediscovered the penetrating writings of two older historians. One was Avery Craven's thesis that abolitionists reacted more to disturbing economic and social change than to slavery itself.[3] The other was Merle Curti's illuminating connection of social class—the mobile middle class in particular—to reform and social improvement.[4] While Craven overplayed the hand of Beardian economic determinism, he broke through the superficialities of sentiment and ideology that clung to the history of middle-class reform efforts. Curti led us to think about the interpenetration of social structure and ideology and culture.

Eric J. Hobsbawm's more recent strategy for writing the history of society resonates with Curti's insights. Hobsbawm's "working plan of social historians" begins with the "material and historical environment," rises through the forces of production and the social relations arising from them, and ultimately arrives at "the shape of the social structure." Thereby, Hobsbawm maintains, the historian will understand the tensions of society during periods of historic change and will be permitted to reveal "the general mechanism by which the structures of society simultaneously tend to lose and reestablish their equilibria." Second, those tensions expose the "phenomena which are traditionally the subject of interest to the social historians, for example, collective consciousness, social movements, the social dimensions of intellectual and cultural change, and so on."[5] Both Curti's and Hobsbawm's insights and analytical prescriptions serve as guides to this exploration of the antislavery rank and file.

The movement to abolish slavery drew ideological inspiration from the Declaration of Independence and especially from its assertion of equality. Sixty years after the insurgent colonists had brought more than a decade of riotous conduct to a peak in the declaration, their descendants adopted more passive tactics to right the wrongs they perceived in the republic. Organization, education, agitation, persuasion, appeals to conscience, and finally political action and the ballot replaced the robust popular confrontations of the 1760s and 1770s.

Although exercising the right of petition pales against the bright flames of a Shays's Rebellion or an anti-Stamp Act shivaree, that right was customary at the birth of the industrial revolution. Petitioning lent itself to wide acceptance and use in the course of popular protest. For the historian the abolitionist petition campaigns provide evidence of the connections between societal changes and the social movement shaping some of those alterations.

This study covers two distinct periods in the antislavery struggle. The 1830s are explored in seven cities: Utica, Rome, and Schenectady, New York, and Fall River, Lynn, Springfield, and Worcester, Massachusetts. Lowell, Massachusetts, was added when usable occupational data showed up in the last stages of the project.

These manufacturing communities were chosen because of the intersection of two modernizing processes: the change to factory production and the emergence of organized antislavery movements. They also seemed to be promising research areas because of the prospect of sufficient data for meaningful quantification. The choice depended on the existence and availability of records. In the course of the work this apparent set of "accidents" provided an automatic and desirable mechanism.

The 1854 petition study adds New Hartford and Ogdensburg, two small towns in upstate New York with a fair amount of available data. It will be dealt with in chapter 8.

When we ask again, Who were the abolitionists? we also ask, Who were their followers? By identifying the men and women who participated in the antislavery petition campaigns we should begin to discern the social composition of that movement. From the emerging profile we shall see their connections with the other reform efforts and principal issues of the day. One of these involved the changing workplace relationships, from locations in artisan workshops and the limited local marketplaces to the more complex ones of the nascent factory system in a national market economy. Another involved the nature and values of the republic that appeared to be headed toward its antithesis, an undemocratic society in which equality would be the principal victim. A third involved the citizenship and status of women as equals with men in American society. Where it has been possible to find direct links between antislavery rank and file and these issues, this study makes them explicit. In the end the social profile of the antislavery rank and file will show that Americans had little stomach for letting the Revolution of 1776 go backward. The antislavery rank and file will be found to reflect American society's travail in a moment of change and impending crisis. Above all, the results of this study are not so indelible or impermeable as to escape tests and challenges. They are welcome.

While I am the author of this work, bearing all the responsibilities for its final appearance, I was in a sense a part of a collective effort. Librarians and research directors of local historical societies have been among the most important of my collaborators. I wish to thank them for their contributions. They are: Douglas Preston, Oneida County Historical Society, New York; Bruce Petronio, Utica Public Library; Elsa Church, Schenectady County Historical Society; Florence C. Brigham, Fall River Historical Society; Nancy H. Burkett, Head of Reader Services, American Antiquarian Society, Worcester; Jessica S. Goss, Worcester Historical Museum; Elizabeth Baxter, City Historian of Ogdensburg, New York; Persis Boyesen, Ogdensburg Public Library; Mary Smallman, St. Lawrence County Historical Society, Canton, New York; Eleanor Vorse and Kathy LaClair, Crumb Memorial Library, State University College, Potsdam, New York; the staffs of the public libraries (reference departments) in Fall River, Lynn, Springfield, Worcester, Utica, Rome, and Schenectady, and of the New York State Library, Albany, New York, and the State Historical Society of Wisconsin, Madison.

A special word of thanks is due to George P. Perros, Legislative and Diplomatic Branch, National Archives, for his cordial and excellent professional collaboration in furnishing the

petitions used here; and the Clerk of the House of Representatives for permission to consult them.

Tax records were provided thanks to the kindness and co-
operation of the Utica Public Library, City Clerk of Ogdensburg, City Clerk of Lynn, County Clerk of St. Lawrence County,
New York, Theresa A. Murphy of Yale University for those of
Fall River, and Nancy Burkett for those of Worcester. Census
records for Schenectady were consulted through the courtesy
of the County Clerk of Schenectady County. F. Shirley Flu-
bacher of the Savings Bank of Utica helped me to review records of the bank's depositors in the 1830s.

Church records were provided by many institutions and their
pastors, to whom I am grateful for enthusiastic help: Father
Flanagan, St. Mary's Catholic Church, Utica; the Catholic Di-
ocese of Ogdensburg; Thyra J. Foster, New England Yearly
Meeting of the Society of Friends; in New Hartford, New York,
Rev. Richard L. Manzelmann, pastor of the Presbyterian
Church, and Robert Anderson, Baptist Church historian, and
St. Stephen's Protestant Episcopal Church; in Ogdensburg,
United Methodist, St. John's Episcopal, and the Presbyterian
churches; in Schenectady, First Baptist Church; in Rome, First
Presbyterian, First Baptist, St. Peter's and St. Mary's Catho-
lic churches, First United Methodist, and St. Andrew's Epis-
copal Church; in Springfield, Saxton Fletcher, historical com-
mittee of First Church (Congregational), Edward Blount, First
United Universalist Church, and First Park Memorial Baptist Church; in Worcester, Dr. Leslie Johnson, Wesley United
Methodist Church, First Unitarian Church, and American
Antiquarian Society; the Congregational Library, Boston,
Presbyterian Historical Society, Philadelphia, American Baptist Historical Society, Rochester, New York, and the Library
of the Theological School, Boston University.

My use of a computer for this project was made easier by
the patient and thoughtful guidance of Claude Lee LaBarre
of the computer center, State University College, Potsdam, New
York, and Brenda Bergstrom of the same center.

Scholars who read, commented upon, and criticized my work
at various stages have my deepest gratitude, even if I may
have stubbornly stuck to my own emphases or phrasings. They
are David B. Davis, Betty Fladeland, Michael A. Gordon, Alan

M. Kraut, Donald M. Scott, Jama Lazerow, Robert Schwartz, and Sanford Schram.

My special thanks are offered to colleagues who very generously sent me materials from their banks of data and copies of their own work for me to use, or pointed out sources helpful to me: John Jentz, Reinhard O. Johnson, Judith Wellman, Thomas Dublin, Theresa Murphy, Ronald Formisano, Patricia Heard, Ellen Henle, and Bruce Levine.

Undergraduate students helpful in my research and who did much of the encoding of data for the computer program were more valuable than they may realize. I thank Nancy Virgil, Nancy Mancini, David Voorhees, Peter Cipperly, Norman Garrett, Phyllis Hadzima, and Camille Cinquina.

I am grateful for a research fellowship granted by the University Awards Committee/State University of New York Research Foundation. It enabled me to visit repositories and to purchase microfilms of city directories and censuses in the summer of 1978.

My most important, influential, clear-minded, and dedicated co-worker is my wife, Miriam Sper Magdol. She has been researcher, editor and proofreader, and consultant par excellence through years of affectionate collaboration.

EDWARD MAGDOL

Madison, Wisconsin
September 1984

NOTES

1. Betty Fladeland, "Who Were the Abolitionists?" *Journal of Negro History* 43 (April 1964): 99-115.

2. David Brion Davis, *Ante-bellum Reform* (New York: Harper and Row, 1967), p. 10.

3. Avery Craven, *The Coming of the Civil War* (New York: Charles Scribner's Sons, 1942), chap. 6, passim; and "An Unorthodox Interpretation of the Abolition Movement," *Journal of Southern History* 7 (February 1941): 57-58.

4. Merle Curti, *The Growth of American Thought* (New York: Harper and Row, 1964), pp. 289-95.

5. Eric Hobsbawm, "From Social History to the History of Society," in Felix Gilbert and Stephen R. Graubard, eds., *Historical Studies Today* (New York: W. W. Norton and Co., 1972), pp. 12-13.

The Antislavery Rank and File

CHAPTER 1

The Background of Abolitionism

Before traveling it is well to know the lay of the land. These first pages attempt to furnish a social and intellectual topography on which to locate the points of an expedition back to the 1830s when the abolitionist movement rose on America's social and political horizon. They also prepare the ground for a look at the negative response to the Kansas-Nebraska Act in 1854, when Free Soilism continued to influence public policies.

During the first two decades of the nineteenth century, as Great Britain, France, and the United States shed mercantilism and donned the garments of industrial capitalism, the movement for emancipation emerged throughout the Atlantic world. Industrialization's powerful energies and its almost insatiable demands for commodities were beginning to remake the material world and at the same time were beginning to remold the leading ideas of Western mankind.[1] Slaves were freed by law and by voluntary manumission from Vermont to the Carolinas; Caribbean slave uprisings, pressing the doctrines of natural and equal rights and the glory of the French Revolution, had already succeeded in the 1790s; and the United States and Britain had banned the international slave trade by 1808.

These events were visible reflections of the hopes of eighteenth century religion and philosophy. Republican virtues seemed triumphant over aristocracy and special privilege. In Britain and America individual salvation, release from predestination, and democratization of church governance were accompaniments of profound economic change. Moreover, Anglo-Americans cheered on Latin American revolutions sweeping away vestiges of Old World Iberian domination and abolishing slavery in the process. The notion of "free labor" fell into place in the minds of some Americans as a "natural" and leading one.

Ironically, yet another aspect of eighteenth century thinking tended to obstruct the displacement of slave labor with free. The rapidly expanding textile factory system, in Manchester, England, for example, and in Rhode Island and Massachusetts in this country, represented a great maw that had to be fed by raw cotton. Eli Whitney's cotton gin facilitated harvesting and marketing, thus stimulating the production of ever larger crops. Even as the use of the cotton gin encouraged manufacturing and the growth of free labor in British and New England factories, it also served to recall the slave labor system back from a path to obsolescence.

Beginning in about 1812 visions of elevation to planter status had sent thousands of small farmers into frontier Alabama, Mississippi, and Arkansas. Upper South planters abandoned worn lands to seize the opportunities oozing from Gulf states' earth. By 1819 a new South was emerging based on a revitalized slavery; by 1820 the slave system pressing on the Louisiana Territory precipitated a crisis over Missouri. Instead of the egalitarian rural republic of Jeffersonian vision, slavery now seemed on the verge of becoming dominant in the whole country. Jefferson voiced fears that the republic would be destroyed in a conflict over slavery. The crisis was postponed and the future freedom of the territory, except for Missouri, was guaranteed by the Compromise of 1820. This was to become an article of faith and an inviolable pact until the Kansas-Nebraska Act.[2]

Yet even at that time blacks doubted the durability of the arrangement. In the decade that followed, both slave and free blacks struggled to abolish the slave system. One means was by conspiracy and revolt, as in Denmark Vesey's foiled slave uprising in 1822. Only five years later the first independent black newspaper in the land was established in New York City by two free black men, John Russwurm and Samuel Cornish. Called *Freedom's Journal*, its declared aim was to achieve the education and elevation of free blacks and to express, at the same time, sympathy for "our brethren who are still in the iron fetters of bondage." A far more militant and exhortatory statement came two years later in Boston when David Walker published his fiery pamphlet, *David Walker's Appeal*. This black militant's call to arms to fight "in the glorious and heavenly cause of freedom and of God" alarmed Southern slaveowners. The threat became all too real in 1831 when Nat Turner led his fellow slaves in an uprising that convulsed slaveowners throughout the South.[3]

Such demonstrations of black initiative in the post-compromise decade undermined an effort by slaveowners and their Northern collaborators to remove free blacks from the United States to Africa. This "African Colonization Movement" would encompass any newly emancipated slaves as well as those blacks now free. Such colonization fit nicely into the concepts of gradual emancipation that dominated antislavery thought in the first quarter of the nineteenth century. But Vesey, Walker, Turner, and *Freedom's Journal* became a vanguard in a renewed and more popularly based struggle to hasten the abolition of slavery, make equal rights a living reality, and overcome white racism.

Events of 1830 and 1831 dramatically strengthened the slaveowners' belief that they were under attack. South Carolina's effort to assert state rights as superior to federal law and its threat to secede from the Union shocked Northerners, offended most of the South, and created a political and constitutional crisis. Tariff measures favoring Northeastern manufacturing interests were preceived as an assault on the planters' power. The Nat Turner uprising, the internal challenge posed by the Virginia legislature's debates over slavery, and President Jackson's threat to use federal troops in upholding federal over states' rights contributed to Southern fears.

Moreover, the appearance in Boston in 1831 of the militant abolitionist newspaper, *The Liberator*, under William Lloyd Garrison's editorship gave no comfort to the slaveowners. In the same period were the slave revolts in Jamaica and the growth of a massive West Indies abolitionist movement in England. These events must have seemed even more ominous to the slaveowners than the 1787 constitutional debates and the 1820 Missouri Compromise discussions.

The most serious challenge to the planters, however, arose from Northeastern American society, its economy, and its liberal ideology. While the new industrial system promised a horn of plenty, it also produced an arena of social discontent centered in the factory. Industrialization further brought a growth of urban squalor, disruption of rural stability, increased migration between country and city, and the great treks westward. Men and women in the North, witnessing new social problems, became "dangerous" social reformers. Others, sparked by Charles G. Finney's religious revival movement, exerted their moral and ideological powers to retain domination over the poor, the infirm, the impious, some of the new manufacturing upstarts (formerly "mere mechanics"), and the new factory laboring class. Thousands accepted personal responsibility for salvation and sin. Soon, the immediatist temper of the social and religious movements was adopted by men like Garrison. This new surge of activism fed into the Garrisonians' disillusionment with the gradualist approach of colonization. Much of American abolitionists' inspiration came from the British abolitionists' stunning achievements. Garrison, along with the wealthy New York merchants Arthur and Lewis Tappan and their followers on the eastern seaboard, merged the ideals of the Enlightenment and immediatism, republican virtue and social responsibility, and Christian righteousness and fervor, with feats of organization and communication. They adopted modern methods of media saturation using pamphlets, tracts, newspapers, and corps of lecturers who became grist for the propaganda mill of their antislavery organization.[4]

Like Johnny Appleseed, antislavery advocates sowed the seeds of state and local societies across the North. The New

England Anti-Slavery Society, established by both whites and blacks in 1832, immediately undertook to combat colonization. In 1833 they joined forces with the New York Anti-Slavery Society, which was influenced by the philanthropic and pious Tappan brothers and their supporters. The charismatic Theodore Weld, a convert to Finney's revivalism, won converts in turn to the abolitionist movement. As part of his "band of seventy," they propagandized and proselytized for the American Anti-Slavery Society, which had been organized at Philadelphia in 1833. In an era of change that loosened the cement of social order, these modern missionaries grasped modern means of suppressing sin, which they saw personified more by aristocratic slaveowners than by any other element of the social scene. Their rhetoric blended some of the more pessimistic tones of evangelism with the optimistic accents of republicanism.

The risk of disharmony among abolitionists could not be avoided in their organizational union. However, where the conventional histories of abolitionism show contention, dissension, and irreparable schisms, Ronald G. Walters's recent analysis demonstrates more unity than division in the movement. That unity was expressed in the Philadelphia convention and in the Anti-Slavery Society's Declaration of Sentiments. Three strands of abolitionism coalesced at the meeting. These were the nonresistant Garrisonians, the evangelicals such as Weld and the Tappans, and the "politicals" who would emerge more prominently in the late 1830s and during the 1840s. Despite their claims to avoid force and to use moral suasion only, the abolitionists clearly intended to use political (and therefore what they considered to be coercive, forceful, and resistant) means. At the same time the political abolitionists retained the rhetoric and the spirit of moral suasion. In the end, the boundaries between the factions appeared to have been blurred. Unity was further demonstrated in the steady growth of state and local membership that crossed the lines of politics, religion, color and class. In 1838, James G. Birney, the society's corresponding secretary, reported more than 1,300 locals, containing 109,000 members, in groups extending from the Northeast to Ohio. They were clustered in and around Boston, Providence, western Massachusetts, New York City and the Mohawk Valley upstate, and from settlements bordering Lake Ontario to Buffalo. In Ohio, the Western Reserve and southwestern river towns were strong abolitionist territories. In Pennsylvania the western border with Ohio was another such stronghold. In the East, Philadelphia was the center of a thriving Quaker and black abolitionism.

The progress of local organizing provoked violent attacks from anti-abolitionist mobs. These opponents were usually "gentlemen of property and standing" who feared "amalgamation" of whites and blacks and were eager to guard the status quo. In Utica, New York, a mob broke up the October 1835 New York State Anti-Slavery Society's convention. In other cities and in many smaller centers anti–abolitionists heckled and attacked antislavery gatherings and mauled abolitionist lectures. The antislavery newspapers, in particular, were the targets of destructive raids, culminating in the murder of Elijah P. Lovejoy in Alton, Illinois, in 1837. Two years earlier, in Boston, Garrison had to be rescued from an attempted lynching. In Cincinnati the press that printed Birney's *Philanthropist* suffered destruction by a mob. Southern and federal authorities participated in this assault on civil liberties by their censorship of the mails which carried antislavery newspapers.

Violence did not seem to daunt the abolitionists. However, the movement faced a crisis by the end of the 1830s. The strategy of moral suasion had failed to budge slaveowners into voluntarily manumitting their human chattel. While a half-million Northern citizens signed antislavery petitions, many more millions failed to do so. The movement had failed to sway the Protestant churches into active and outspoken opposition to slavery despite the many activists in their midst.[5] The crisis was intensifed by struggles of Anti-Slavery Society leaders over tactics. Issues such as the role of women in the movement and the role of party politics divided them.

The abolitionists were forced to seek alternative institutional and ideological means to gain power and execute reforms. Despite the early violent and hostile rejection of antislavery activities, a growing and more visibly tolerant public opinion suggested resort to a political party as the logical and effective alternative to exhausted moral suasionism. Beyond the abolitionists' own small organized circles the tactic of partisan political action was showing signs of acceptance. By 1835 hundreds of thousands were signing antislavery petitions. Additional encouragement came when a number of office seekers responded favorably to the abolitionists in their districts. Among them were Ohio's Whig Joshua R. Giddings and Democrat Thomas Morris, New York's Seth Gates and Vermont's William Slade. John Quincy Adams and some of his Massachusetts colleagues in the House flooded it with their constituents' petitions. But neither Adams nor most of the others were abolitionists. An exception was Representative Nathan B. Borden of the Fall River district, the "Quaker hatter," who was a member of the local antislavery society.[6]

A potentially large sector of the public wished to protect the abolitionists' civil rights. This was made evident in the widespread condemnation of both the murder of Elijah Lovejoy and the mob's destruction of his newspaper presses. Similarly, public opinion supported the right of petition in defiance of the congressional gag rule. The Western Reserve voters, in a special election, returned Giddings to the House of Representatives after it had censured him and forced his resignation. Giddings had won his seat on the strength of his opposition to the gag rule and his antislavery commitment. He repaid his constituents by continued antislavery leadership in the Congress for a generation. Finally, in the 1840s he and his colleagues succeeded in rescinding the gag rule.[7]

As tactical priorities were being reordered, men like Birney, Alvan Stewart, Henry B. Stanton, William Goodell, and Gerrit Smith saw a need to accept the reality of male suffrage. A new direction was charted in the late 1830s with the decision to establish the Liberty party. Although of necessity it appealed to male voters, the party's activity did not diminish the Garrisonian abolitionist commitment to women's rights or stop the active roles of women in the abolitionist movement. On the other hand support for the Liberty party grew, in small steps to be sure, despite the split over political action and women's rights at the 1840 convention of the American Anti-Slavery Society.

The departure into politics did not, however, assure smooth traveling. It took a succession of third parties—Liberty, Free Soil, and Free Democratic—to set the stage for the Republican victory in 1860. Antislavery party growth was slow in the early1840s, seemed to explode in 1848 with the election of Free Soil Senators and Representatives, and then virtually became nonexistent in 1853. Political abolitionists accommodated their platform to voter interests and to coalition expediencies. This caused the third–party movement to moderate radical demands for the abolition of slavery into a plank simply against its extension into the territories. The move was accompanied by virtual silence on the issue of equal rights for blacks. It also required that the antislavery party broaden the platform to encompass reform and economic measures responsive to the interests of farmers, mechanics, manufacturers, and others. Anti-extensionism gained wider support as it became linked with the idea of an insatiable "slave power" conspiring to swallow up all free institutions. The meteoric Free Soil party was the principal beneficiary as both Whigs and Democrats split their ranks over this issue in 1848. Its Liberty party predecessor, campaigning solely for abolition and black equality, had attracted a mere 7,000 votes on its first try in 1840; and increased only to 65,000 four years later. The annexation of Texas, the outbreak of war with Mexico, and the failed Wilmot Proviso exposed the party's futility. But by 1848 the Free Soil party, led by former Democrat and former President Martin Van Buren, received 291,804 votes. A dozen new representatives were elected, but when Whig and Democratic party leaders read the signs and declared for non-extensionism, they stole the Free Soil party thunder and robbed it of a future beyond 1849.[8]

After the major parties hastened to cut their losses in 1848, a deceptive calm fell upon the national debate over slavery. The Compromise of 1850 was a patchwork, or a rattling omnibus settlement sure to collapse at the first bump in the road. One impediment to the compromise was the inclusion of the inhuman fugitive slave law. The act was abhorrent and provocative to Northerners. If it did not make abolitionists overnight it did arouse thousands to heed the abolitionist message.

Two years later Americans were brought closer to the movement by the electric effect of Harriet Beecher Stowe's novel *Uncle Tom's Cabin*. The book's details of the indignities and brutalities of slavery helped to tear down the facade of resignation and accommodation to the Compromise of 1850. Mrs. Stowe helped immensely to awaken latent mass antislavery sentiments. Within a year after Stowe's smashing success, politicians tried to revive the Free Soil party as a new Free Democratic party, hoping to harvest a bumper crop of new-grown antislavery cadres.

The new party came on the scene too late to capitalize on Mrs. Stowe's proding of the antislavery conscience. The Free Democratic vote in the 1852 presidential election was small and disappointing. A ray of hope did shine through the meager poll, however, when, with John P. Hale leading the ticket, the party's vote increased by 150 percent over Birney's 1844 Liberty party results. Free Democrats were further encouraged by the demise of the Whig party in a contest marked by apathy toward the major parties. In the 1853 state elections the new party scored impressive gains in the Middle West, but it was forced into difficult and losing contests in Maine, Vermont and Massachusetts. On the whole, Free Democrats were heartened by the Whig crossovers and local alliances with their candidates in Ohio and Wisconsin. A new force in party politics seemed to be in the offing.

The sleeping giant of public opinion awoke with a great leap in 1854. Senator Stephen A. Douglas of Illinois and others proposed the Kansas-Nebraska bill. It would permit slavery's extension into the Louisiana Territory north of the 1820 compromise line. If major party fragility was exposed in the 1848 defection to Free Soilism, the Kansas-Nebraska Act helped to complete the process of erosion and to promote new party alignments. The territorial issue transcended partisan interests and redirected national attention to principles rather than expedients. The stunning Northern opposition to Douglas's proposal was grounded in the belief that the Missouri Compromise was an inviolable contract. The Kansas-Nebraska Act was deemed contrary to its letter and spirit. On a deeper level the Act appeared to close the gates of opportunity and freedom opened by the Declaration of Independence and the Revolution of 1776. It was these ideals that were the ultimate cultural resources of most mid–nineteenth century Americans.

Protests against the act drew thousands of people to mass meetings from Boston to Milwaukee. Voluminous petitioning of Congress reminiscent of the massive campaigns in the 1830s revealed the breadth and depth of an antislavery constituency that had grown over a generation. Some abolitionists drew contrary lessons from the Kansas-Nebraska controversy. Garrisonians renewed and reiterated their denunciation of the Union and its Constitution as proslavery and prayed for its dissolution. Their perfectionist impulses led them to abandon hope in a world of compromise and ambiguity. Political abolitionists, on the other hand, having endured almost two decades of isolation and frustration, hastened to consolidate the gains of 1854. They undertook to revitalize politics and launched anew the effort to bring the nation back on the track of the Declaration of Independence. Old Liberty party stalwarts led an enlarged antislavery constituency into a coalition with a wide set of groups representing midcentury manufacturing and farming interests. The antislavery crusade had entered the mainstream of American politics. Its constituency, built in only one generation, was by far the largest of the antebellum social reform efforts.

While historians have devoted significant attention to abolitionist leaders, they have largely overlooked the men and women who were the backbone of the movement. The rank and file abolitionists deserve a long overdue recognition and consideration. They are the subject of this book.

NOTES

1. David Brion Davis, *The Problem of Slavery in the Age of Revolution* (Ithaca, N.Y.: Cornell University Press, 1975), reviews the ideological ambiguities of emergent laissez-faire capitalism in the

United States, Great Britain, and France and their transatlantic dependencies.

2. Clement Eaton, *The Growth of Southern Civilization, 1790–1860* (New York: Harper and Row Torchbook, 1963).

3. Herbert Aptheker, ed., *Documentary History of the Negro People in the United States*, vol. 1 (New York: Citadel Press, 1951), pp. 84, 95; John Hope Franklin, *From Slavery to Freedom* (New York: Alfred A. Knopf, 1974); August Meier and Elliott Rudwick, *From Plantation to Ghetto* (New York: Hill and Wang, 1975); William Freehling, *Prelude to Civil War: The Nullification Controversy in South Carolina, 1816–1836* (New York: Harper and Row Torchbook, 1968).

4. David Brion Davis, ed., *Ante–bellum Reform* (New York: Harper and Row, 1967); Louis Filler, *The Crusade Against Slavery, 1830–1860* (New York: Harper and Row Torchbook, 1960); Merton L. Dillon, *The Abolitionists: The Growth of a Dissenting Minority* (DeKalb: Northern Illinois University Press, 1974); James Brewer Stewart, *Holy Warriors: The Abolitionists and American Slavery* (New York: Hill and Wang, 1976); Russel B. Nye, *Fettered Freedom: Civil Liberties and the Slavery Controversy, 1830–1860* (East Lansing: Michigan State College Press, 1949); Aileen S. Kraditor, *Means and Ends in American Abolitionism: Garrison and His Critics on Strategy and Tactics, 1834–1850* (New York: Pantheon, 1969); and Ronald G. Walters, *The Antislavery Appeal: American Abolitionism after 1830* (Baltimore: The Johns Hopkins University Press, 1976). These works provide rich narrative and interpretation of the reform and antislavery movements dear to the hearts of nineteenth century middle–class social critics and activists. The text of my essay here and in the following paragraphs depends on them and on my own assessments.

5. Members of those churches had plunged into energetic abolition activity, but the weight of habit and expediency on the churches was ironical. The revivalism of the 1820s had replenished church membership and had generated a potential army for social reform. Abolitionists, believing that the churches had squandered that potential in order to keep their skirts clean of schism and contention, attacked them. Weld and the Grimkes blamed this weakness on clergymen whom they charged with "truckling subserviency to power, . . . [and] clinging with mendicant sycophancy to the skirts of wealth and influence." In Ronald Walters's words, the Protestant establishment became bogged down in "sterile formalism." The religious establishment proved to be resistant to moral suasion for a full decade. In the 1840s it finally revised its position. Walters, *The Antislavery Appeal*, p. 43.

6. Richard H. Sewell, *Ballots for Freedom: Antislavery Politics in*

the United States, 1837–1860 (New York: Oxford University Press, 1976), pp. 47–48; Nye, *Fettered Freedom*, pp. 40–42; Stewart, *Holy Warriors*, pp. 86–87, 106–7; Edward S. Adams, "Anti-Slavery Activity in Fall River," Fall River *Herald News*, February 27, 1939.

7. Stewart, *Holy Warriors*, pp. 86–87, 106–7; Joseph C. Lovejoy and Owen Lovejoy, eds., *Memoir of the Reverend Elijah P. Lovejoy* (New York, 1838).

8. Sewell, *Ballots for Freedom*, passim.

CHAPTER 2

Boom Times in the Northeast: Upheavals Economic and Spiritual

Northern America's entry into industrial and agricultural capitalism occurred during the first four decades of the nineteenth century. It brought phenomenal changes in its train. Factories and factory cities sprang up on countryside crossroads and alongside powerful rivers. Lowell, Lawrence, Waltham, Lynn, Pawtucket, Fall River, Worcester, Chicopee, and Springfield, Massachusetts, and Utica, Rome, Schenectady, Troy, Rochester, and Buffalo, New York, were only a few of the leading urban-industrial centers. Capital took hold of the production of food, goods, and transportation. Northern American culture and society were disrupted. New England women and farm girls became the first factory force. A new man, the merchant capitalist, challenged the older mercantile elite and the clergymen for community leadership. Factories and machines removed control of labor processes from the hands of craftsmen. After a short period merchant capitalists, driven to protect investments and maximize profits, attempted to cut wages. Others resorted to rent increases in company housing. Artisans were forced to compete for work with unskilled children, women, and immigrants. A wedge constructed of piece-rates, speed-ups, and division of labor was driven between master mechanics and journeymen. Factories were eroding the fraternity and harmony of old small-shop relationships.[1]

The unsettling results of early industrialization were intensified by the transportation revolution which lasted from about 1815 to 1860. Successive and overlapping booms in canal building, railroad construction, and steamboating extended the industrial market to the wide-open Western states and territories, Southern plantations, and the region of enterprise between the Great Lakes and the Ohio and Mississippi rivers. Manufacturing and transportation urbanized the nation, setting off a constant flow from country to city, and from town to town. In some New England communities 80 percent of the unskilled laborers, unable to find steady jobs, moved away. Worcester bootmakers and shoemakers out-migration reached 90 percent because mechanized, large-scale factories made steady employment uncertain. In the famed Lowell textile mills, labor turnover of both male and female operatives reached 26 percent in the 1830s. Studies of the nineteenth century directories and censuses show that 40 to 60 percent of the inhabitants of a variety of communities were likely to disappear in the course of a decade. The young men and those who owned no real property matched the unskilled in rates of movement. Smaller proportions of skilled and successful men also moved to seek further economic advantage.[2]

Life and labor in the rapidly expanding cities fell short of the optimistic claims made by manufacturers and other middle-class promoters. Great wealth and the poverty on which it rested were in evidence. Urban crowding was intensified by the increasing number of Irish immigrants hired to build canals and railways, and to work as cheap factory laborers. Boom times from 1827 to 1837 notwithstanding, wages lagged steadily behind runaway prices. By the early 1840s unemployment had struck one-third of the working classes. Farmers and farm laborers, too, who made up the bulk of America's population, faced a hard life in this period. New England farmers, having lost out to Western wheat producers, moved off their lands. In historian Avery Craven's words, "The abandoned farm became a permanent part of the New England countryside."[3]

The great wealth in "the era of the common man" negated Alexis de Tocqueville's egalitarian myth. Abolitionists saw inequality in the rise of an aristocratic slaveowner planter class. Labor reformers identified an economic aristocracy formed by bankers and the owners of factories, mines, and means of transportation. To those reformers, such men seemed too easily to acquire state licenses and charters that gave them monopolies in land, money, machinery, commodities, and labor. Wealth and power seemed to come not from honest hard labor, as of old, but from birth and from a signature on a check or contract. The craftsmen's dreams of becoming independent producers, so exalted in nineteenth century America, were being slowly killed by the new aristocracy.

Social disorders, exacerbated by urban crowding and inequality, stimulated the establishment of reform movements. A temperance movement reflected one such thrust. Drunkenness was thought to reveal a moral breakdown and a breach of social harmony and responsibility. There were also organizations for public schools, peace, prison reform, and equality for women, and against crime, poverty, and Sabbath violations. Churches were subjected to criticism from zealous reformers seeking liberalized doctrine and practice. Prisons, asylums, schools, and regenerated churches were promoted in order to reach the desired goals of religious revival and purified public morality, sobriety, and industriousness. A sign of the unsettled times was offered by Utica, New York aldermen, who passed an ordinance on January 31, 1834, intended to shut down "and control brothels, gambling places, assignation houses, etc." Some reform movements were initiated by worried elites, but they also were adopted by artisans and others in the lower middle classes. Journeymen, mechanics, and laborers could be found actively participating in temperance, school, and prison reform movements.[4]

The producing classes wrote their reformatory and antiaristocratic concerns into the platforms of the Workingmen's parties of the late 1820s and the 1830s. They called for laws to reduce the working day to ten hours, for free public schools supported by taxes, equal taxation on property, and a mechanics' lien law. They also opposed licensed monopolies, imprisonment for debt, unsanitary and crowded living conditions of workers, and the conspiracy laws which were used to outlaw early trade unions. Some local Workingmen's parties expressed anticlerical sentiments and called for electoral system reforms, abolition of capital punishment, temperance, criticism of banks and charitable institutions. They objected to the undemocratic militia system and the complexity of the legal system. Middle–class supporters of some of these planks seemed to share the mechanics' concerns for equity, social harmony, and fidelity to republican ideals. Finally, craftsmen organized trade unions to protect their workplace interests, and women mill workers, especially in Lowell, staged turn-outs against the employers whose profit motivations caused them to cut wages, raise company housing rents, and "rationalize" production.[5]

The 1830s were marked by a high incidence of riots, strikes, and violent attacks against political, social and economic nonconformists. Abraham Lincoln, lecturing in Springfield, Illinois, in 1837, deplored the change in the nation from one noted for law and order into one where violence and disorder had become commonplace. Many groups feared conspiracies. Some of the more prominent suspects were banks, the abolitionists, the foreigners, the Catholics, the Mormons, the Money Power, the Slave Power, and the liquor merchants and distillers. Mobs attacked Mormons and Catholic schools and institutions, as well as the abolitionists.[6]

The turbulence of the 1830s—the most tumultuous decade since the Revolution—has posed an intriguing historical question. Something had occurred to upset a long period of apparent social harmony. Earlier, canal building and extension of the market, relatively easy access to credit and land, and the prospect of a long post-Napoleonic peace must have contributed to the sense of stability and optimism. Now, slavery loomed larger, more expansive and aggressive, factories and cities were displacing the workshops, the craftsmen, and the open spaces, and monopoly and subversion threatened. Optimism and hope for the republic suffered seriously. A recommended restorative was the kit bag full of reform movements. The most prominent of these was the movement to abolish slavery.

A reconstruction of the abolitionist movement's ranks should furnish fresh insights into the history of reform and early

American industrialization. The connections between them will be illuminated by a study of the men and women who signed antislavery petitions and who also joined abolition societies, subscribed to their newspapers, and eventually voted for a succession of antislavery political parties.

The cities in which the 1830s petitioners lived and worked were experiencing a wave of economic expansion and population growth as well as the earliest changes from rural and preindustrial to urban and industrial society. Despite the almost incessant mobility of younger men and women, Worcester nearly doubled its population from 1830 to 1840, and Lynn, Fall River, Springfield, and Utica grew by 50 to 60 percent in that decade. Lowell's booming textile industry stimulated a tripling of its inhabitants. Rome and Schenectady also expanded but at a slower rate, remaining smaller than the others.[7]

These early stirrings of industrial capitalism, and the bustling commercial and transportation activity, changed the physical character of these towns. But more importantly, these social changes, along with the great revivalist stirrings of the times, influenced the way residents viewed themselves and the antislavery movement. Utica, New York serves as an example of this rapid and massive change.

A resident of Utica recalled the frenzied rush to turn rural fields into city commercial and manufacturing blocks. "It is surprising how little of the city has been laid out by corporate action," commented L. M. Taylor in 1886. "A man owns a piece of land more or less," he continued, "has it surveyed, lays out the streets with reference to the shape of the particular property, files his map, and proceeds to sell. The result of this is often confusion. The most as well as the worst of this sort of work was done in 1836–1837. In those wild years large tracts of land in and about Utica were mapped—many times without survey, but from descriptions in the deeds—streets were laid on them, usually without the slightest reference to neighboring property or the character of the land; all being arranged to make the largest number of lots."[8]

This conduct of affairs produced the city's grand thoroughfare, Genesee Street, a broad avenue that arched up the hill from the Erie Canal and ran southwest toward neighboring New Hartford. Banks, stores, insurance offices, workshops, lawyers' and physicians' offices, and some mansions of the rich shared the prospect that focused on the wooded hills to the north and the fields and woods that stretched south. Valuable as frontage on Genesee Street was mistaken to be, belief in it helped to produce the chaos of the back streets where tradesmen, laborers, and magnates resided and some plied their trades. Some roads narrowed to crooked lanes and came to a dead end. Some were permitted to enter Genesee Street at right angles, thus losing the chance to beautify the intersection with a triangular park or other mini-landscaping. Many streets never made connection with the central avenue. Taylor lamented that "the city as a whole has grown up without any general plan devised or enforced by any one."[9]

Utica enjoyed a strategic location on the Erie Canal in central New York. By 1835 it was a city of ten thousand. The carrying trade into the countryside, south via the Chenango Canal and north via the Black River Canal, opened up opportunities for men in commerce, insurance, and transportation, and made this preindustrial town prosperous. Artisans were employed in workshops producing goods from combs to carriages. Craftsmen such as carpenters and caulkers, as well as laborers, constructed canal vessels in two boat-builders' yards and in three dry docks on the Mohawk river.

In the middle of the decade the volume of traffic in and out of the city was evident in the weekly arrival of twenty-eight canal packets and eighty-six stages, as well as in eight wagonmaker shops and three coachmaker shops. By 1838 railroad tracks would pose a threat to these water and wagon arteries and to their accessory businesses. The following decades would see iron horses that galloped as no real ones had, into the north country and downstate toward the developing regional and national markets, via Binghamton, Philadelphia, and Baltimore.

Women worked in the cotton mills of Utica's suburbs and in the city's eleven tailoress shops, in thirty millinery and dressmaker stores and shops, and as "sewing girls" in eight merchant tailor shops. Clothing and feeding Uticans gave employment to butchers, bakers, tailors, and almost fourscore of cordwainers and bootmakers. Sixty-five grocers dispensed drams of hard liquor as well as food and other necessities. Sixty-six blacksmiths, 122 carpenters and joiners, 29 cabinet makers, 33 masons, and 23 painters helped to make the city's construction boom a reality. Among the products of "manufactories" were tinware, thimbles, stoneware, sash and blinds, millstones, copperware, brass and iron from foundries, hats and caps, joiners' tools, morocco leather, and shoemakers' lasts and boot trees. In 1834 printers and editors produced a twenty-one thousand weekly circulation of various newspapers.

Refreshment of the population was furnished in part by two breweries and nine innkeepers, in addition to the groceries that dotted the back streets and neighborhoods where 238 laborers resided. If they were at all like their peers in Rochester, as Paul Johnson has described them, these workingmen dropped in at the local dramshops for the sake of conviviality.[10] This pastime was a part of an autonomous social life separate from that of the new middle class. We have found no similar descriptions for Utica, nor has its most recent and perceptive social historian, Mary P. Ryan, but there is no reason to believe that such customs of preindustrial workingmen were not practiced there.

Nearby villages of Paris, Whilestown, and New Hartford had already introduced cotton and woolen mills which enhanced Utica's role as a financial and shipping center. In the 1840s some of its economic elite were already planning more factories to avoid loss of economic leadership to Rochester and Lockport and to these nearby villages. By 1845 its first steam-driven factory was in operation.

Earlier, in October 1835, many of these same "leading men" had allowed their frustrations to spill over into an organized mob attack on a meeting of the New York State Anti-Slavery Convention. Perhaps their frustration and "embarrassment" were fed by fears of the competition for economic leadership from those other towns. Such concerns may have helped to fuel their hysterical fear of racial amalgamation. But above all they appeared to be furious over the challenge to their authority and leadership by new men and new forces in the nation and the community. The riots probably revealed a deep-seated conflict over differing value concepts between the well-to-do but anxious mob and the antislavery artisans, mechanics, free laborers, shopkeepers, and rising manufacturers.

Prominent among the anti-abolitionists were "the older and more stable of the citizens, desirous to preserve the laws and peace of the country." Among these "gentlemen of property and standing" were some of Genesee Street's proprietors and professionals: Robert S. Lattimore and Abraham B. Williams, draper and tailor with premises at number 85; a short distance back toward the canal were Harvey Barnard, a dealer in paper hangings, and Robert Jones, a grocer and confectioner. One of the wealthiest men in town, John C. Devereux, was part of the angry mob. He was at the time president of the United States Branch Bank located at 122 Genesee Street, as well as the most prominent Catholic layman, active in temperance and other civic affairs. Within two years he would become mayor. Other powerful elite figures were Horatio Seymour, a lawyer and former mayor; Orsamus B. Matteson, a lawyer and for a number of years a state supreme court commissioner; the merchant Ephraim Hart; A. B. Johnson, son of a pioneer merchant, an in-law of the presidential Adams family, president of the Ontario Branch Bank, leading Presbyterian, and advocate of Sunday mail deliveries, then a sensitive issue and a practice offensive to Presbyterian church elders; William Tracy and J. Watson Williams, attorneys; and Justice of the Peace John B. Pease.

A few of the abolitionists were the neighbors—in their businesses and trades—of these leaders. Interspersed among them on Genesee Street one could find these victims of the mob's fury: Samuel Lightbody, who owned a hide and leather store; James C. DeLong, morocco leather manufacturer and leading Methodist, soon to be an alderman in the city council; Oren Clark and George Brayton, merchants; Philip and Ira Thurber, grocers; the dry-goods merchants James W. Doolittle, and Spencer Kellogg and his sons; Jacob Vanderhyden, cordwainer; and Henry N. Newland, who made and sold boots and shoes. The riot victims included as well the Reverend Beriah Green, head of the Oneida Institute and the man who was responsible for the introduction of organized antislavery activity in Whitesboro and Utica. Fellow victims were the Reverend Oliver Wetmore of the Presbyterian Church, and the prominent attorney and abolitionist spokesman, Alvan Stewart. The depth of feeling displayed by the mob may be appreciated in the fact that Wetmore's son Edmund was one of the respectable mob that attacked the convention site, the Bleecker Street Presbyterian Church. On the other hand it is notable that "respectable mechanics" made a last-ditch effort to avert the riot when they met in the courtroom on October 20 "in favor of free discussion and supremacy of the laws." But even this gathering was disturbed and threatened with violence. It was forced to "adjourn prematurely." Thus the old elite imposed its rule over law by a resort to lawlessness in their anxiety to keep Utica safe for commerce and progress as they saw it.

Despite this upheaval in the life of the city, Utica remained a stronghold of antislavery sentiment in central New York. Less than six months later, Theodore Weld, the indefatigable evangelist and abolitionist organizer extraordinary, came to Utica and delivered a series of sixteen lectures to overflow crowds. At this early 1836 revival there were no respectable gentlemen mobs to menace Weld. He was spared the harassments he would later experience at Troy and other lecture sites. Weld's fervent style and the acuity of his argument were eminently persuasive, as the mass response to him indicated. Six hundred names were reported to have been added to the membership of the Utica Anti-Slavery Society. An antislavery petition of March 12, 1836, containing twelve hundred names, "a majority of them men" and "probably a majority of the legal voters," was sent to Congress praying for the abolition of slavery in the District of Columbia. This was a stunning act in the drama of social change. It signalled the coming victory of the new middle class. And it contributed to the tension created by the contest over leadership of culture and society between nascent manufacturing capitalism and the older mercantile and genteel elite.[11]

Utica maintained the pattern of urban and radical vitality that had made the city an upstate hub of social reform, reli-

gious revival, temperance, and the anti-Masonic and Workingmen's party movements in the 1830s. None of the others
equalled the electric effect of Utica's waves of revivalism, as
the city grew from frontier village into bustling canal town
and finally into the metropolis of a regional factory-town network.

Like Rochester and a host of other towns from Oneida county
to Buffalo, Utica felt the heat of Charles G. Finney's evangelism from 1825 to 1831. People were swept into a new sort of
religious fervor. Out of the searing experience western New
York became known as the "burned-over district." Finney's
attack on outmoded Calvinism was a counterpart to the Jacksonian attack on the fetters to economic opportunity and social equality. It was thus no accident that in the wake of the
Erie Canal's penetration of central and western New York in
1825, there should also be a moral penetration of old ways
and institutions on behalf of the new American bourgeois.
Finney's six-month Rochester campaign in 1831 linked individual moral reform to the social force of the temperance
movement and helped to revitalize Presbyterian, Baptist, and
Methodist churches. In Utica and many other places Finney's
lectures on individual responsibility for salvation and re-
demption sent hundreds into these "pietistic" churches and
also into the antislavery movement.

When Finney evangelized Utica in 1826, only a year after
the opening of the Erie Canal, he was enthusiastically received. The city had been prepared by other revivals in 1814
and in 1819. In this campaign, seven years later, middle-class
men and women responded as in the past, but now, so did a
minority of the new factory working class in the vicinity. When
he preached his liberal Protestant creed with its democratic
and antiaristocratic overtones to the employees and masters
of the New York Mills, converts from these audiences provided immediate growth in Methodist churches.

The warmest reception of Finney's appeal seemed to be more
in manufacturing centers like the Utica region, Rochester, and
Lockport, than in purely commercial ones like Albany, Syracuse, and Buffalo. As Whitney Cross found in his landmark
study of western New York's evangelical religions, there was
a connection between Finney's campaigns of the 1820s and

1830s and the manufacturers, master craftsmen, and journeymen in the emerging factory towns.[12]

Utica's antislavery movement was only one—but a major—aspect of the drive to extirpate sin and find security and spiritual refreshment amid the falling stones of Calvinism and under the dangling double-edged blade of economic progress. On one edge were Jacksonian-era optimistic expectations of economic opportunity; on the other, pessimistically, was the threat that these would be severed by monopoly and privilege. Finney tended to instill self-confidence in men and women facing a new way of life. Hence, in Utica, for example, the growth of the pietistic churches (largely by women converts), a spreading temperance movement, and an influential religious missionary press went hand in hand with the city's antislavery sensibility.

These movements were energized by Finney's new creed of individualism and man's capacity for inner perfection. He left a lasting imprint on Utica, as he would five years later in his phenomenal revival in Rochester. The results of his teachings rebounded to the benefit of manufacturers, upwardly mobile master craftsmen, and some merchants and skilled wage earners. He provided a world view that embraced the sobriety and self-discipline necessary to steady the nerves and the consciences of employers and to induce free-spirited, intemperate celebrants of St. Monday to mend their ways and conform to their interests. At the same time many wage-earning skilled workers maintained their own temperance societies and joined in other moral reform efforts out of a sense of responsibility, self-discipline, and self-improvement, in part stimulated by Finney's lawyerlike arguments and exhortations.

Utica was well on the way to cosmopolitanism and diversity in the 1830s. Its American-born population was gathered not only from Oneida County towns and nearby counties such as Madison, Herkimer, and Otsego, but from New England states as well. Its foreign born were mainly from the British Isles. Welshmen became a prominent contingent with a distinctive culture and language. Men and women from other European lands were here from the beginning of the century but none were so numerous as the Welsh. Irish Catholic laborers who had built the canal made up another distinctive group; other

Irishmen such as the wealthy John Devereau had succeeded in attaining commercial and financial heights and leadership in the city. The Welsh were active Baptists and Presbyterians. They supported the temperance and antislavery movements. Representative of their men who signed the March 1836 antislavery petition were Owen Owens, a baker located at 10 Main Street, and David E. Morris, a cordwainer and sexton of the First Presbyterian Church. Owens was a member of the Second Baptist Church. Morris also was active in the Welsh Temperance Society of Utica and its vicinity.

The part of Utica's labor force that came from Welsh immigrant ranks was enlarged by letters encouraging kinsmen and friends to come across the Atlantic. As John Lewis wrote to his nephew in 1832, "There are many new roads and canals being built in every corner of the country giving plenty of work for everyone. We would advise all our countrymen to come over. . . . thousands of our brethren from the north [of Wales] come here and to Steuben during the three or four months of summer." Lewis added that Utica could be attractive because of its three Welsh churches and forty Welsh preachers. Such a welcome mat probably made Utica irresistible. Here were promises of comfort for a migrant's body and soul.[13]

Utica seemed to be freeing itself from old ways and to be ever on the move—on the canal and the river to the north; up and down Genesee Street, the nerve center of commerce, finance, and nascent industrialism; along the back streets where houses seemed to burst up from the ground; along the wagon-laden roads that ran into the countryside. In such a bustling atmosphere of economic activity, religious reawakening, fluid social relations, demographic diversity, and signs of political radicalism, the idea of human bondage and its possible extension became increasingly unpalatable.

NOTES

1. George Rogers Taylor, *The Transportation Revolution 1815–1860* (New York: Harper Torchbooks, 1968), and Thomas C. Cochran, *Frontiers of Change: Early Industrialism in America* (New York:

Oxford University Press, 1981); John R. Commons and others, *History of Labour in the United States* (New York: The Macmillan Company, 1916), vol. 1, and Philip S. Foner, *History of the Labor Movement in the United States* (New York: International Publishers, 1947), provide the bases for understanding America's industrial revolution, which are summarized here and in the following pages. See also Herbert G. Gutman, *Work, Culture and Society in Industrializing America* (New York: Alfred A. Knopf, 1976), for a refreshing view of working-class culture and consciousness during a century and a half of industrial capitalism.

Finally, in order to comprehend the mentalities of artisans undergoing the first aggrandizements of capital on their domain, see a highly sophisticated interpretation by Sean Wilentz, "Artisan Republican Festivals and the Rise of Class Conflict in New York City, 1788–1837," in Michael H. Frisch and Daniel J. Walkowitz, eds., *Working-Class America: Essays on Labor, Community, and American Society* (Urbana: University of Illinois Press, 1983).

2. Robert V. Wells, *Revolutions in Americans' Lives: A Demographic Perspective on the History of Americans, Their Families, and Their Society* (Westport, Conn: Greenwood Press, 1982), pp. 111–13; Robert Doherty, *Society and Power: Five New England Towns, 1800–1860* (Amherst: University of Massachusetts Press, 1977), chap. 4 (pp. 30–45), pp. 54–55; Jonathan Prude, "The Social System of Early New England Textile Mills: A Case Study, 1812–40," in Frisch and Walkowitz, eds., *Working-Class America*, pp. 19–26.

3. Edward Pessen, *Jacksonian America: Society, Personality, and Politics* (Homewood, Ill.: The Dorsey Press, 1969), pp.47–48; Avery Craven, *The Coming of the Civil War* (New York: Charles Scribner's Sons, 1942), p. 127.

4. David Brion Davis, ed., *Ante-bellum Reform* (New York: Harper and Row, 1967), especially the articles by Davis, Joseph R. Gusfield, and John L. Thomas.

5. Edward Pessen, *Most Uncommon Jacksonians: The Radical Leaders of the Early Labor Movement* (Albany: State University of New York Press, 1967); Pessen, "The Workingmen's Party Revisited," *Labor History* 4 (Fall 1963): 203–26; Maurice F. Neufeld, "Realms of Thought and Organized Labor in the Age of Jackson," *Labor History* 10 (Winter 1969): 5–43.

6. David B. Davis, "Some Themes of Counter-Subversion: An Analysis of Anti-Masonic, Anti-Catholic, and Anti-Mormon Literature," *Mississippi Valley Historical Review* 47 (September 1960): 205–24; Leonard L. Richards, *Gentlemen of Property and Standing: Anti-*

Abolition Mobs in Jacksonian America (New York: Oxford University Press, 1970).

7. The remainder of this chapter relies upon local histories and especially upon the work of the new social historians.

Useful for my understanding of Utica and Rome history were: Richard L. Ehrlich, "The Development of Manufacturing in the Erie Canal Corridor, 1815–1860" (Ph.D. dissertation, State University of New York at Buffalo, 1972); *Report of the Committee Appointed to Investigate Motive Power of Water and Steam as Applicable to Manufacturing* (Utica, 1845); Mary P. Ryan, *Cradle of the Middle Class: The Family in Oneida County, New York, 1790–1865* (Cambridge: Cambridge University Press, 1981); John Martin Roberts, "The Social Dimensions of Urban-Industrial Structure: Evangelical Religion, Reform and Economic Growth in Oneida County, New York" (Paper presented to Brockport, New York, Conference on Political and Social History, 1973); Judith Wellman, "The Burned-Over District Revisited: Benevolent Reform and Abolitionism in Mexico, Paris, and Ithica, New York, 1825–1842" (Ph.D. dissertation, University of Virginia, 1974); Moses M. Bagg, ed., *Memorial History of Utica* (Syracuse, N.Y., 1892); Henry J. Cookinham, *History of Oneida County*, 2 vols. (Chicago, 1912); Daniel E. Wager, ed., *Our City and Its People: A Descriptive Work on the City of Rome, New York* (Boston, 1896).

On Schenectady: A. A. Yates, *Schenectady County, New York: Its History at the Close of the Nineteenth Century* (1902); George Rogers Howell, *History of the County of Schenectady from 1662 to 1886* (New York: Munsell, 1886); Joel H. Monroe, *Schenectady Ancient and Modern* (Geneva, N.Y.: W. F. Humphrey, 1914).

On Ogdensburg: P. S. Garand, *The History of the City of Ogdensburgh* (Ogdensburg, 1927) (The spelling discrepancy is due to a modernization that dropped the "h" in the twentieth-century version of the city's name.); Harry F. Landon, *The North Country. A History Embracing Jefferson, St. Lawrence [and other] Counties, New York*, 3 vols. (Indianapolis, 1932).

8. L. M. Taylor, "The Streets of Utica," *Transactions of the Oneida Historical Society at Utica, 1885–1886*, no. 3, p. 41.

9. Ibid.

10. See Paul E. Johnson, *A Shopkeeper's Millenium: Society and Revivals in Rochester, New York, 1815–1837* (New York: Hill and Wang, 1978), pp.55–61.

11. John L. Myers, "The Beginning of Anti-Slavery Agencies in New York State, 1833–1836." *New York History* 43 (April 1960): 171.

12. Whitney R. Cross, *The Burned-Over District: A Social and In-*

tellectual History of Enthusiastic Religion in Western New York, 1800–1850 (Ithica, N.Y.: Cornell University Press, 1950), chapters 4–5.

13. John Lewis to an unidentified nephew, February 28, 1832, in Alan Conway, *The Welsh in America: Letters from the Immigrants* (Minneapolis: University of Minnesota Press, 1961), pp. 65–66.

producing textiles, a wire manufacturing mill, an iron foundry, seven large machine shops, and two paper factories. In addition a variety of factories in surrounding villages and towns such as Millbury, Southbridge, Northborough, West Boylston, and Harvard contributed to the county's rich industrial diversity.

By the mid-1830s Springfield was markedly industrialized and the sixth most populous town in Massachusetts. The value of its man-made products was third highest in the state. One rather large enterprise was the federal Armory established in 1795. It began with forty employees, and by 1850 more than three hundred men turned out the famed Springfield muskets. Women in the families of some of the Armory's mechanics and machinists were among the earliest Connecticut River valley factory operatives in the nearby Chicopee and Cabotville cotton mills. Springfield itself had seven cotton mills that rested on an investment of $1.7 million.

Fall River's transformation from preindustrial port village at the mouth of the Taunton River into a restless factory city may also represent what occurred in Lynn, Worcester, and Springfield during the 1830s. One writer referred to Fall River as "a city of the wilderness, rising in the midst of hills, trees, and water-falls and rural scenery. . . . Industry is the presiding goddess of Fall River; an idle man could no more live there than a beetle in a bee hive."[2] Amid the sylvan and riparian treats offered by the broad river and the high cliffs that contained it, now sprawled cotton manufactories, a calico works employing 300 hands, iron works and nail factories, and a machine shop. Most of the factories were constructed across the high rocky sides of a deep black gulf through which waterfalls rushed to Mount Hope Bay. By 1833 the streets came alive with people patronizing about one hundred shops and stores.[3] In the next few years banks, newspapers, homes, boarding houses, and churches filled in more and more of the land lining the river, the creeks, and the ponds that furnished water power for the new economy. By the time a statistical survey of Massachusetts industry was compiled in 1837, Fall River's ten cotton mills employed 638 females and 337 males. The mills ingested 1.5 million pounds of cotton annually and the workers and their machines turned out 7.7 million yards of cloth worth $668,000. In the two print works, 500 employees printed 12 million yards of cloth worth $1.6 million. Other relatively large enterprises were the nail factory (40 employees whose product's value was $260,000); a whale fishery (120 workers employed on six vessels which delivered 105,000 gallons of whale oil and sperm oil); and a woolen mill in which eight sets of machinery were worked by 120 operatives (65 male, 55 female). Twenty-two hands at the rolling and slitting mill converted iron into 3,000 tons of hoops and rods; and an equal number of mechanics manufactured $10,000 worth of machinery. Smaller establishments, with from 4 to 40 workers, produced boots and shoes, hats, chairs, cabinets, leather, and brass, copper, and tinware.[4]

The reliance of cotton manufacturers on the putting-out system, by which the home became a workshop, is illustrated by the April 1835 payroll book of one company, the Anawan Mill. Among the 268 names—spinners, carders, cloth dressers, machinists, and other workers—only seven weavers were listed. A local historian explains their small number in this cloth-producing mill by reminding us that "much of the weaving was still done in the homes of the village and on the farms across the river." Such a system of domestic production also provided cheap labor for Lynn's shoe manufacturers. A wide network of women shoe binders in the families of artisans received uppers to be sewn by them and returned to the shoe bosses for shoemaking. By 1833, wage-earning women shoe binders, paid by the merchant capitalist or manufacturer, numbered 1500 in Lynn alone. Women in nearby Essex county towns and in New Hampshire villages and farms were similarly drawn into the new economy along with their menfolk. By 1837 female shoe producers in their outwork system (15,366) outnumbered the women and girls (14,759) in the cotton textile mills of Massachusetts.[5] But in the textile towns such as Fall River, Springfield and Chicopee, and Lowell, female workers were drawn into the factories. In Fall River, for example, within a few years "you could hardly have found a loom in anybody's home. The mills had taken over."[6]

At the head of this process of change were men of skill,

vision, capital, and boldness, risking their own resources and those of hundreds of other people. Lowell's industrial elite were Boston capitalists seeking to improve upon the dismal English manufacturing scene. With fortunes amassed in mercantile enterprises, they increasingly spread capital throughout New England, from Chicopee to Maine and New Hampshire. They were, as one historian says, "both capitalists and concerned citizens, hard-dealing merchants and public spirited philanthropists, entrepreneurs and ideologues."[7]

These Boston associates were absentee owners of a vast manufacturing domain over which they ruled and within which they were allied with local counterparts. In Worcester the latter were men like Ichabod Washburn, founder of the city's wire industry, temperance advocate, philanthropist, and promoter of schools and other civic improvements. Edward Earle, secretary of the Worcester Anti-Slavery Society, was an iron dealer who also managed a saw mill and owned a flour and grain business. This member of a well-known Quaker family became a selectman and later mayor of Worcester. Alpheus Merrifield, whose name heads the list of men endorsing the Worcester Anti-Slavery Society's constitution, was a wealthy carpenter and builder. Similarly, the president of the Utica Anti-Slavery Society was Asaph Seymour, iron foundry proprietor and member of an old and prominent Oneida County family. The president of the Wesleyan Anti-Slavery Society of the Methodist Episcopal Church, who was also a member of the New York State Anti-Slavery Society's executive committee, was James C. DeLong, manufacturer of morocco leather and a wool dealer. And at least one member of the Oneida County society's executive committee was an artisan, the cordwainer S. H. Sheldon. Clergymen, grocers, druggists, merchants, and a lawyer, as well as numerous craftsmen, served as secretaries, as vice presidents, as executive committee members, and on boards of managers of the city, county, and state Anti-Slavery Societies and of the local Wesleyan Methodist antislavery organization. Other leaders were mechanics and rising manufacturers; some had moved in from the farms. They shared Washburn's optimistic values for the molding of society along the lines of moral material progress.

The temperance movement found considerable support among them, as it aimed to promote sobriety, industriousness, economic regularity, and dependability.[8]

In Lynn, two kinds of entrepreneurs led the transformation from small shop to factory. At first, merchants tried to control shoemaking by furnishing raw materials to individual cordwainers in their small shops. The merchants then sold the finished pairs of shoes to dealers and shopkeepers. This method failed because it lacked control of the production process. The merchants were replaced by "shoe manufacturers" many of whom were former master shoemakers. They were "tough, austere, methodical and ambitious" men who established central shops with the aid of credit from wealthier capitalists. As bosses in these workshops they directly controlled the production process, the raw materials, and the marketing. Like their Worcester counterparts they attempted to impart to journeymen and laborers the ideals and values of "industrial morality" and of "a well regulated republic": self-reliance, sobriety, hard work, obedience to superiors, and self-discipline. Boss and journeyman within this moral industrial world also shared a belief in "the mutuality of their interests."[9]

This is not to say that life always conformed to the harmony rhetoric. As the sociologist T. H. Marshall observed, "sectional co-operation between labour and capital does not render impossible or unnatural a general antagonism between labour and capital."[10] Within the shared world view of boss and journeyman friction and conflict broke out. One hundred seventy–three strikes occurred nationally between 1833 and 1837. Wage cuts, rent increases without pay increases, and speeded-up machinery aroused mill workers to protest and to go into the streets. Carpenters, shoemakers, and tailors struck against employer attacks on their customary control of work, wages, and hours. A pioneering New England textile-mill strike broke out in Pawtucket, Rhode Island, in 1824. Ten years later men and women unsuccessfully walked out at the Lowell mills, and in Dover, New Hampshire factories. Lynn's female shoe binders also struck in 1834. In 1836 the Lowell workers, led by militant mill "girls", reorganized and won a big strike.

Nationally, strikes and defiance of capitalist exuberance and exploitation made the manufacturers' talk of harmony appear quite hollow and self-serving. Legal obstruction of labor's efforts to organize, as in the case of the Geneva boot and shoemakers in 1835–36, was only one example of class contradiction. A court found the working men guilty of violating a conspiracy statute because "they tried to prevent other journeymen from working for less." This decision aroused profound resentment and wide condemnation from workingmen who perceived the trial as evidence of antirepublicanism and the overweening arrogance of the new aristocracy.[11] Such republicanism was echoed in George Bancroft's Fourth of July address to Springfield Democrats, in which he labeled the Whigs the party of vested rights, and maintained that the Whig himself "pants for monopoly." At the beginning of the 1830s Springfield Democrats had already denounced the "small band of loungers and Springfield aristocrats . . . the ruffle shirt party."[12]

Efforts to resist manufacturer economic and social hegemony were further exemplified by the Fall River Mechanics' Association establishment of a workers' cooperative store as an alternative to company stores and the paternalism that spawned them. Still another demonstration of class disharmony was the workers' ten-hours movement of the 1840s, which, however, included middle-class allies. The Fall River abolitionist, Reverend Asa Bronson, pastor of the First Baptist Church and vice president of the Bristol County Anti-Slavery Society, became a staunch defender of the workers' claim to a shorter day. Bronson, a man "of most massive proportions," was forced out of his pastorate in 1844 for his pro-labor activity by "a few of our aristocratic manufacturers, who love wealth more than justice." He quickly moved to establish the Second Baptist Society in 1846.[13]

Co-founder of the Baptist Society with Bronson was John C. Milne, who served as its clerk and treasurer. Milne was an editor and printer, and had been a frequent signer of antislavery petitions during the 1830s. He probably was a leading figure in the Anti-Slavery Society, although this cannot be documented. He became an advocate of other progressive causes such as a free homestead law and wage-lien laws. Milne referred to capitalists as "a miserable race of parvenus, parasites and popinjays" and as men who "hated everything connected with labor, except its dividends."[14]

Despite such sharp cleavages, manufacturers and working people did agree in their opposition to slavery. Workers' spokesmen, however, developed an independent line of argument from that of their middle-class colleagues. George Henry Evans, speaking in 1831, maintained that the republican concept of equal rights so deeply cherished by Jackson era artisans and tradesmen could never become reality as long as two million humans were held in slavery. Evans rallied freemen and equal rights advocates to link their own struggles with the fight to abolish slavery. Five years later, George Gunn, an Philadelphia labor leader, transmitted to American workers the antislavery appeal of the Chartist Workingmen's Association of England. The communication asserted that black bondage could not be in the interest of all workers. Instead, the appeal said, "This degrading traffic" in human beings was in the interest of "those who . . . would equally sacrifice to their love of gain and mischievous ambition, the happiness of either black or white."[15]

If the hundreds of artisans and factory operatives who signed antislavery petitions in the late 1830s had heard or read the English appeal, we have no evidence of a direct connection between the two actions. We do know that in Lowell and Lynn, women weavers, spinners, and machine tenders added their signatures to the petitions. Lynn's male cordwainers by the hundreds also supported the abolitionist appeals; in particular, leaders of the Journeymen cordwainer society, at odds with the shoe bosses, signed petitions and were members of the Lynn Anti-Slavery Society.

Hundreds of the female shoe binders, who organized their own union in 1833 to resist shoe manufacturers' wage cuts in Lynn and Saugus, probably were among the city's 912 female antislavery signers of a December 1838 petition. Two of those women led the binders in the Lynn Female Society and the Saugus Female Society and were members of the Lynn Female Anti-Slavery Society. They were Miriam B. Johnson, treasurer of the Lynn group, and Martha B. C. Hawks, vice president of the Saugus organization. Like hundreds of their sisters in the Lowell mills, these Lynn working women supported abolitionism. One may have the impression that the Lowell mill operatives, already under the heavy hand of their employers' paternalism, seemed compelled to sign the "paper" that "the owners of the factories hand round . . . for the girls to sign against black slavery in the South."[16] But paternalistic duress can hardly explain the women laborers' response. Their own experience in the mills persuaded them that their employers treated them like slaves and led them to identify readily with the condition of chattel slavery. These Lowell women seemed no more the supine subjects of their employers than the Lynn shoe workers. Their 1836 walkout in Lowell, at virtually the same time that hundreds signed antislavery petitions, belies any docility attributed to them on either issue—wages or human bondage. Their invocation of the American Revolution and its ideals to justify their strike, and their abhorrence of slavery, advertised their sophistication, discernment, class awareness, and female-consciousness. These first members of the industrial working class, whether in Lynn, Lowell, Springfield, Chicopee and Cabotville, Fall River, or Worcester, in Vera Shlakman's words, "had recognized the analogy between their position and that of the chattel slaves."[17]

By the mid–1840s, the labor spokesman William West of Boston was reminding readers of *The Liberator* of the need to abolish "all slavery, both chattel and wages."[18] Lowell manufacturers, lawyers, and other middle-class antislavery leaders could not accept such a slogan.

Significant and complicated social and industrial relationships between manufacturers and laborers and artisans were thus dramatized in the intersection of the antislavery movement and the new classes forming during the New England industrial revolution. Fluid, seemingly egalitarian conduct of daily life in the preindustrial world of these Northeastern cities was fondly and charmingly recalled by late nineteenth century writers indulging in what seems a surfeit of nostalgia. For example, Johnson's *Sketches of Lynn* and the series of newspaper articles in the *Lynn Record* of the 1880s recalled the sometimes carefree days of the town, and the unregimented work, play, and discourse in old-time Lynn shoe shops. The stories were replete with the colorful personalities and the folkish wisdom of the 1820s and 1830s—before the shoe factories came in meaningful numbers. A Springfield historian also recalled happy times in an era preceding and during the erection of imposing cotton and woolen mills, paper factories, and other havens of power-driven machinery. One reads these sympathetic and nostalgic accounts of life in preindustrial towns, always aware of the undertone of longing for its possible return. Nevertheless, some of the chroniclers "balance" the picture by celebrating the "progress" their cities have achieved by the time in which they write—the era of steam power and mature industrial capitalism of the 1880s and 1890s.

Much truth resides in the remembrance of harmony between manufacturers and craftsmen, operatives, and common laborers. But, though such nostalgic works avoid or "forget" the strikes and discontentments of the workers in their exultation over progress, conflicts did occur and must be appreciated as a hallmark of industrial capitalism.

On the whole, the heritage of republican values appeared to transcend emerging class divisions. The same heritage was claimed by both men of property and economic power and by artisans, mechanics, and factory workers. Those republican values and virtues were the grounds on which they stood together against chattel slavery. Class alliances in antislavery organizations and activities rendered early American industrialization and the society of manufacturing towns more complex—simultaneously more harmonious and more divided—than if they had not been held in the tension between republican ideals and the transforming forces of nascent industrial capitalism.

NOTES

1. Unless otherwise noted, this chapter derives from the following studies. On Massachusetts cities: Adna Ferrin Weber, *The Growth of Cities in the Nineteenth Century: A Study in Statistics* (New York, 1899).

On Fall River: Alice Brayton, *Life on the Stream* (Fall River, 1962);

Frederick M. Peck and Henry H. Earle, *Fall River and Its Industries* (Fall River: B. Earl and Son, 1877); Frank W. Hutt, ed., *A History of Bristol County*, 3 vols. (New York: Lewis Historical Publishing Co., 1924); Henry Fenner, *History of Fall River* (New York: F. T. Smiley Pub. Co., 1906); John T. Cumbler, *Working-Class Community in Industrial America: Work, Leisure, and Struggle in Two Industrial Cities, 1880–1930* (Westport, Conn.: Greenwood Press, 1979) (Lynn and Fall River).

On Lynn: Alonzo Lewis and James R. Newhall, *History of Lynn, Essex County, Massachusetts* (Boston: John Shorey, 1865); David N. Johnson, *Sketches of Lynn: The Changes of Fifty Years* (Lynn: Thomas Nichols, 1880); Paul Faler, "Workingmen, Mechanics and Social Change: Lynn, Massachusetts, 1800–1860" (Ph.D. dissertation, University of Wisconsin, 1971); Alan Dawley, *Class and Community: The Industrial Revolution in Lynn* (Cambridge: Harvard University Press, 1976).

On Springfield: Michael H. Frisch, *Town into City: Springfield, Massachusetts, and the Meaning of Community, 1840–1880* (Cambridge: Harvard University Press, 1972); Vera Shlakman, *Economic History of a Factory Town: A Study of Chicopee, Massachusetts*, Smith College Studies in History (1934–35); Mason A. Green, *Springfield, 1636–1886, History of Town and City* (Springfield, 1888).

On Worcester: Charles Nutt, *History of Worcester and Its People* (New York: Lewis Historical Publishing Co., 1919); William Z. Lincoln, *History of Worcester* (Worcester, 1862); Caleb A. Wall, *Reminiscences of Worcester from the Earliest Period* (Worcester: Tyler and Seagrave, 1877); Charles C. Buell, "The Workers of Worcester: Social Mobility and Ethnicity, 1850–1880" (Ph.D. dissertation, New York University, 1974); Joshua Chasan, "Civilizing Worcester" (Ph.D. dissertation, University of Pittsburgh, 1974); Ian R. Tyrell, *Sobering Up: From Temperance to Prohibition in Antebellum America, 1800–1860* (Westport, Conn.: Greenwood Press, 1979).

On Lowell: Thomas Dublin, *Women at Work: The Transformation of Work and Community in Lowell, Massachusetts, 1826–1860* (New York: Columbia University Press, 1979; originally Ph.D. dissertation, Columbia University, 1975); John F. Kasson, "The Factory as Republican Community, Lowell, Massachusetts," chap. 2 in *Civilizing the Machine: Technology and Republican Values in America, 1776–1900* (New York: Grossman, 1976).

2. Peck and Earle, *Fall River and Its Industries*, p. 186.

3. Catherine R. Williams, *Fall River, An Authentic Narrative* (Boston: Lilly, Wait & Co., 1834), pp. 10–13, 16–17.

4. Erastus B. Bigelow, *Remarks on the Depressed Condition of Manufacturers in Massachusetts, with Suggestions As To Its Cause and Its Remedy* (Boston: Little, Brown and Company, 1858).

5. Mary H. Blewett, "Work, Gender, and the Artisan Tradition in New England Shoemaking, 1780–1860," *Journal of Social History* 17 (Winter 1983): 225, 229.

6. Brayton, *Life on the Stream*, p. 53.

7. Kasson, *Civilizing the Machine*, p. 71.

8. Tyrell, *Sobering Up*, chap. 5; city directories of Utica (1837–38) and Worcester (1845); American Anti-Slavery Society, *Second Annual Report* (Boston, 1835); biographical files at American Antiquarian Society, Worcester, Massachusetts; *The Friend of Man*, October 27, 1836, May 31, 1837, November 29, 1838; Constitution of the Worcester Anti-Slavery Society (ca. 1839–40).

9. Faler, "Workingmen, Mechanics and Social Change," pp. 49–53, 203, 215; Dawley, *Class and Community*, chap. 1, "The Entrepreneurs," pp. 11–41; Dawley and Faler, "Working-Class Culture and Politics in the Industrial Revolution: Sources of Loyalism and Rebellion," *Journal of Social History* 9 (June 1976): 467–68; Paul Faler, "Cultural Aspects of the Industrial Revolution: Lynn, Massachusetts, Shoemakers and Industrial Morality, 1826–1860," *Labor History* 15 (Summer 1974): 367–94.

10. T. H. Marshall, *Class, Citizenship and Social Development* (Westport, Conn.: Greenwood Press, 1963), pp. 166–67.

11. John R. Commons and others, *History of Labour in the United States*, vol. 1 (New York: Macmillan, 1916), pp. 381–411.

12. Green, *Springfield, 1636–1886*, pp. 437, 442.

13. Edward S. Adams, "Anti-Slavery Activity in Fall River," Fall River *Herald News*, February 17–28, 1939, and in typescript at Fall River Historical Society; *The Friend of Man*, June 30, August 25, 1836; Fall River *Mechanic*, September 28, 1844; *The Liberator*, November 23, 1838.

14. Bernard Mandel, *Labor: Free and Slave* (New York: Associated Authors, 1955), p. 144.

15. Ibid., p. 71.

16. The source of this quote could not be found. (M.S.M. and M.G.)

17. Vera Shlakman, *Economic History of a Factory Town: A Study of Chicopee, Massachusetts* (New York: Octagon Books, 1969), p. 61.

18. Quoted in Aileen S. Kraditor, *Means and Ends in American Abolitionism: Garrison and His Critics on Strategy and Tactics, 1834–1850* (New York: Vintage Books, 1967), p. 249.

CHAPTER 4

Men Who Joined Abolitionist Societies

It is no surprise to find the antislavery movement developing rapidly in many Massachusetts and New York communities. In the antebellum period a developing "free labor" ideology embraced not only a harmony of interests but a shared repugnance of slavery. Membership counts in local antislavery societies were particularly high in Worcester County and in the city of Utica, 551 and 550 respectively.[1]

Worcester County abolitionists were divided into a northern division and a southern division. Both regions were dotted with societies in villages and small towns. The northern group, including Fitchburg and Leominster, included a membership of 290, most of whom were women. The southern division Anti-Slavery Society, which embraced towns like Holden, Harvard, and Millbury, reported a membership of 261 in 1838. Stephen and Abby Kelley Foster and Adin Ballou are only three of its more famous and colorful leaders. Ministers like George Allen, manufacturers like William B. Fox, and the Quaker editor of the Massachusetts *Spy*, John Milton Earle, played less bombastic but steady leadership roles.[2]

Abolitionism in Utica and its environs was sparked by some of the nation's most important advocates of immediatism. The local antislavery society benefitted from the magnetism of

Theodore Weld's lectures, delivered in early 1836. Hundreds attended his series of sixteen talks and hundreds in the overflow crowds were turned away. Here, too, William Goodell established the antislavery newspaper, *The Friend of Man*, and Alvan Stewart, a wealthy abolitionist attorney, orated vigorously against slavery. In neighboring Whitesboro, the Reverend Beriah Green headed the manual labor school, Oneida Institute, where both Weld and the future black leader Reverend Henry Highland Garnet were among the students. Clergy and laymen from the city's Methodist and Presbyterian churches functioned in the Wesleyan Methodist Anti-Slavery Society as well as in the city and state nonsectarian societies. It was fitting that so vibrant an abolition center should be chosen the site of the 1835 New York State Anti-Slavery convention. At the state meeting a year later, six Utica abolitionists were elected to the executive committee, and Utica men filled the posts of vice president, corresponding secretary, recording secretary, and treasurer.[3]

The year 1834 was one of active antislavery organization in Fall River, Massachusetts. The antislavery auxiliary society was organized that year and grew rapidly. By 1837–38, it reported 279 members. A female society, also established in 1834, reported a membership of 175 a year later. The First Baptist Church, under the leadership of its courageous radical abolitionist pastor, the Reverend Asa Bronson, proved to be a home for antislavery organization. In that same year the local society was established there at a huge meeting of one thousand persons with Bronson elected its president. He and the outspoken Methodist minister, the Reverend Phineas Crandall, were elected executives of the large and energetic Bristol County Anti-Slavery Society, which included the whaling port of New Bedford, another abolitionist hotbed. Quaker families, such as the Buffums and Chaces, played leading roles in these organizations despite a Society of Friends ban on nonsectarian activity.[4]

In Lynn, Massachusetts, a white benevolent society called The Lynn Colored People's Friend Society had been founded in 1832. Its purposes were to abolish slavery, gain equal "civil privileges and natural rights" for blacks and Indians, and improve free blacks' "character and condition." Its officers included shoemakers, shoe manufacturers, and a teacher. The pastor of the Second Methodist Society of Woodend, a neighborhood of journeymen cordwainers, became its president. Lynn's Anti-Slavery Society, which enrolled 272 male members between 1832 and 1834, was also led by craftsmen and manufacturers, with the Quaker shoe manufacturer William Bassett its 1841 president. He had gained notoriety among Friends because of his public defiance of the ban on joining "worldly" organizations when he became a member of the American Anti-Slavery Society in 1835.[5]

Less is known of the abolitionist local auxiliaries in Rome and Schenectady, New York, and Springfield, Massachusetts. Rome's antislavery society was led by the Reverend Arba Blair and appears to have acted in concert with Utica's organization. The Rome society reported 184 members in 1836. Because we lack independent histories of the Rome and Schenectady locals, it is not possible to describe their daily activities. However, we do know that in the latter city local craftsmen and manufacturers were among its officers. Sidney Ross, the president, was a coachmaker. Among its five vice presidents were Albert Brown, cabinetmaker, R. P. G. Wright, a hairdresser, and John P. Beckley, merchant tailor. Faculty members of Union College were also prominent in the society's affairs.[6] A similar "respectable" element led Springfield's antislavery society. The Congregational minister, The Reverend Samuel Osgood, devoted his time and efforts, and those of his church, the First Church of Springfield, to the antislavery cause. He and two other clergymen were the vice presidents of the Hampden County Anti-Slavery Society, which held its first annual meeting at First Church in January 1838. Osgood's home was a station on the escaped slave's Underground Railroad. Later, out of Springfield's tiny black community came John Brown's militant League of Gileadites, defiant of the fugitive slave law.[7]

What can be learned about the rank and file of these organizations? A list of subscribers to the Worcester Anti-Slavery Constitution (undated but about 1838–39) and a list of names entered in the "Minutes Book of the Lynn Anti-Slavery Society from 1832 to 1839" have been linked to occupational data. Information was found for 48 out of 92 of the first group and for 126 out of 257 of the second. Table 4–1 shows the number and percent of men in nine occupational groups. The relatively high proportion of skilled men, who probably included masters and wage-earning journeymen, corresponds to the equally high ratios of skilled men in the occupational structure of contemporary manufacturing and workshop towns. In the city of Schenectady, in 1841, the skilled men dominated the others with 52.3 percent. In Utica, in 1837, 42.6 percent of the males in the labor force were skilled. In a comparable male structure in Lynn, in 1841, skilled workers, including masters, were 66.8 percent. Cordwainers accounted for 64 percent of the city's male workers in 1832, and 46 percent in 1841. We can therefore safely estimate that shoemakers were at least half of the city's employed male population in the mid- or late 1830s. They should and do dominate in antislavery society membership.

Closely related to those in the skilled category are the seventeen manufacturers among the men in group 3 in Table 4–1: proprietors, managers, and officials. Fourteen of them were Lynn shoe manufacturers owning only a modest amount of real property. Those for whom tax assessments were found are concentrated in the category I have designated as the middle level, where the worth of real property is from $501 to $5,000. Six of them owned real estate valued between $1,001 and $5,000; four owned from $501 to $1,000. These shoe manufacturers may have been those energetic and resourceful men just starting out in their rise toward wealth and power. They would soon control hundreds of workers and tens of thousands of dollars in capital equipment. Two examples of such men among the abolition society members were Nathan Breed and Christopher Robinson, eventually to become capitalists with wide-ranging possessions and enterprises in Lynn in railroads, wharfs, insurance companies, and other manufactures. Robinson began his career in about 1808 as an apprentice shoemaker at the bench in Micajah Newall's workshop. By 1822 he had acquired capital and materials and employed twelve shoemakers and twelve binders in his own central shop.

Table 4–1
Occupations of Antislavery Society Members
Lynn and Worcester, 1830s

Occupational Group	LYNN (N)	%	WORCESTER (N)	%	TOTALS (N)	%
1. Unskilled & Menial Service	1	.8	1	2.1	2	1.1
2. Semi-Skilled & Service	2	1.6	2	4.2	4	2.3
3. Proprietor-Manager-Official	20	15.9	12	25.0	32	18.4
4. Skilled	88	69.8	24	50.0	112	64.4
5. Commerce & Sales	4	3.2	2	4.2	6	3.4
6. Semi-Professional	1	.8	1	2.1	2	1.1
7. Professional	2	1.6			2	1.1
8. Farmers	2	1.6	6	12.5	8	4.6
9. Miscellaneous	6	4.8			6	3.4
Totals	126		48		174	

Thereafter he suffered the effects of a relatively volatile industry buffeted by depression and boosted by expanding markets. Despite business failures in the panic of 1837 he displayed the skill and resiliency to bounce back in the 1840s.[8] Nathan Breed, scion of a well-to-do Quaker clan, was born to property and by midcentury had made good use of it to become one of Lynn's wealthiest capitalists.[9] In 1832 he employed more than two hundred men and women. At least four other Breeds were also shoe manufacturers. Stephen N. and Joseph III were among the leading members of the Anti-Slavery Society. Bartlett B. was one of the signers of a call to a convention of Christian ministers and laymen, and one of T. N. Breed's employees, Richard Tufts, was a leading member of the Lynn Colored People's Friend Society. Both Breed and Robinson demonstrated strong support of republican values when they became active in the antislavery society.

Many artisans joining in this endeavor owned little property. In this regard they shared the lot of most Americans. More than one-third of the skilled men in the sample illustrated in Table 4–1 held no assessable real estate in 1837. This is quite similar to the situation of all the Lynn rate payers, 61 percent of whom were propertyless in 1832 and 56 percent of whom remained in this position in 1837. In contrast, 80 percent of the proprietors-managers-officials category in the sample did own assessable real estate.

The contrast of economic circumstances among members of abolition societies is further illustrated by statistics of personal property ownership. Most of the artisans held no personal property at all. Among the remainder, possessions might include a horse, a vehicle, domestic animals, a savings bank account at interest, insurance, or the tools of their trade. At first glance there would seem to be some equality with proprietors-managers-officials, for a number of them were in the same low status of personal property holdings. However, whereas about one-third of the entrepreneurs owned from $1,001 to $5,000 worth, only 2 percent of the skilled men were in this property category. Class identities arising from these property-owning distinctions serve to emphasize that a commitment to abolitionism was not confined to the middle-class intellectuals, professionals, and men of property.

In Lynn, working-class abolitionism is revealed in a new and striking way that affirms Thomas Wentworth Higginson's recollection of his "cheerful yesterdays." In the 1830s, cordwainers began to perceive the first cracks in the structure of harmony guiding their relations with masters and bosses. As central shops were taken over by entrepreneurs, their interests diverged from those of the wage earners. The journeyman's concern turned toward self-definition and self-organization.

Despite their differences, cordwainers were more than amply represented in the abolition society membership list and on antislavery petitions. This is illustrated by comparing those documents with the list of "ward and commissioned" officers of the Lynn Mutual Benefit Society of Journeymen Cordwainers.[10] This wage-earner society was organized in the 1830s as a collective response to wage cuts and to prices charged in the stores owned by shoe manufacturers. A reserve fund was created to aid members and to extend support to the female shoe binders who had also organized for the same purposes. Above all, Society spokesmen asserted their class interests in trying to win "the full value of their labor." Although membership lists are unavailable, the names of the officers are known. William Phillips, chairman, and Richard S. Ham, secretary, were signers of antislavery petitions between 1836 and 1838. Eight members of the twelve-man committee on objectives that met on January 1, 1834, also signed petitions. And, of the sixteen ward committeemen, nine joined the others in signing petitions for the abolition of slavery in the District of Columbia and for denial of Texas's admission as a slave state in the Union. In sum, nineteen of the twenty-nine known cordwainer activists are found in this sampling of antislavery petitioners. Ten of the twenty-nine, with William Phillips among them, were *members* of the Lynn Anti-Slavery Society.[11]

Workingmen in Rochester, New York, provide a western comparison to their east coast peers in the antislavery constituency. A recent study of 302 moral suasionist (Garrisonian) and political (Liberty party) abolitionists in this Genesee valley city in the 1830s and 1840s finds important class differences in the composition of the two schools. Middle-class men in professional and proprietor groups provided 53 percent of the Garrisonian faction. Working-class men in all skill categories comprised 54 percent of the politicals. Similar and related class divisions occurred in the Rochester temperance movement. Workingmen were inclined toward the secular appeal of the Washingtonian societies. Middle-class temperance men responded to the sin-laden message of religious social reformers. As to their church affiliations, Rochester Garrisonians tended to belong to evangelical churches which had been affected by the Finney revival. Large portions of so-called "blue collar" men in political and moral suasion ranks were not identified with any church: half of the moral suasion manual workers, and 68 percent of the political artisans and laborers. Significantly, the sample of Rochester's undivided abolitionist constituency revealed 40 percent in working-class occupations and 42 percent in so-called "white collar" positions. The politicals among them were secular, working-class, and obviously in the democratic mainstream. The moral suasionists tended to have an opposite set of characteristics.[12]

These differences reflect the social and ideological changes accompanying early industrialization in western New York. The revivalism of the "burned-over district" had burned itself out by the early 1840s. Secular temperance appeals paralleled Liberty party antislavery economic arguments linked to workingmen's interests. Political consensus against the expansion of slavery was growing. Factories displacing workshops spurred capitalist optimism. Working-class wariness and self-assertion, rooted in equal rights republicanism and mechanic-class interests, confronted rationalization of industry and profit-maximization. The tenets of equal rights that inspired the pronouncements of Lynn shoemakers and other mechanics against monopoly and aristocratic privilege also embraced abhorrence of slavery. The statistical data presented here suggest that these principles impelled a significant number to join the Lynn and Worcester Anti-Slavery Societies and the Liberty party in western New York. Given the similarities in social structure, economic change, and republican culture, there is good reason to consider the two Massachusetts societies and the Rochester abolitionist rank and file as prototypes of New York and Massachusetts manufacturing communities.

NOTES

1. American Anti-Slavery Society, *Annual Reports* for 1835, 1837, 1838; James Eugene Mooney, "Antislavery in Worcester County: A Case Study," (Ph.D. dissertation, Clark University, 1971) pp. 42–48.

2. Ibid.

3. American Anti-Slavery Society, *Third Annual Report* (Boston, 1836).

4. Edward S. Adams, "Anti-Slavery Activity in Fall River," Fall River *Herald News*, February 17–18, 1939, and in typescript at Fall River Historical Society; *The Liberator*, November 23, 1838; *The Friend of Man*, June 30, August 25, 1836.

5. Lynn City Directory, 1832 and 1841; Record Book of Lynn Anti-Slavery Society, 1832–1839 (Lynn Historical Society).

6. American Anti-Slavery Society, *Third Annual Report* (Boston, 1836).

7. Mason A. Green, *Springfield, 1636–1886, History of Town and City* (Springfield, 1888), p. 442.

8. Paul Faler, "Workingmen, Mechanics and Social Change: Lynn, Massachusetts, 1800–1860" (Ph.D. dissertation, University of Wisconsin, 1971), p. 150.

9. Ibid., p. 147.

10. Lynn *Record*, January 8, 1834.

11. Record Book of Lynn Anti-Slavery Society.

12. James L. McElroy, "Social Reform in the Burned-Over District: Rochester, New York As A Test Case, 1830–1854" (Ph.D. dissertation, State University of New York at Binghamton, 1974), pp. 168–73.

CHAPTER 5

The Petitions and the Rank and File

The main sources of this antislavery profile are the petitions sent to Congress in the 1830s.[1] They addressed three issues: (1) abolition of slavery in the District of Columbia and the United States Territories, (2) admission of new slave states and the annexation of Texas, and (3) the congressional gag rule that tabled antislavery petitions and blocked discussion of their contents on the floor of Congress. The main source of the later antislavery profile is a similar outpouring of memorials and petitions in 1854 against the extension of slavery and the abrogation of the Missouri Compromise.

There are other sources, of course, that aid in identifying individuals in the antislavery constituency. One is the membership list of abolition societies discussed in chapter 4, with which one may compare the antislavery constituency at large. Another is voter lists compiled in the small towns of Harvard and Northborough in Worcester County, Massachusetts. These permit an unusual opportunity to identify Whig and Democratic antislavery men. Finally, a massive female antislavery petition of fourteen hundred Lowell signatures permits a new view of the movement's rank and file women.

The entire body of the petitions in the National Archives has singular value for this reconstruction. It constitutes an immense record of abolitionism's supporters. Some two million names were gathered in the 1838–39 campaign of the American Anti-Slavery Society. This stunning job was performed by about thirteen hundred local societies with only about one hundred thousand members.[2] The petitions may also be regarded as a powerful political voice accessible to both men and women long before the victory of female suffrage. These records fill the void left by the absence of poll books and poll lists, which might have revealed voter preferences and their ideals and interests. Moreover, the lists of petitioners on this as on other public questions remain valuable opinion surveys for the historian. Citizens took this First Amendment right seriously, for the journals in each session of the legislature contain many entries of petitions for internal improvements, social reforms, economic policies, and individual claims. They may be linked to such social and economic data as city directories, censuses, church membership lists, tax assessors' lists of ratepayers and polls, and company payrolls, as they have been in this book. The process yields the major components of a social profile: occupation, age, birthplace, church affiliation, and property ownership.

A major source of the petition activity of the 1830s lay in the widening antislavery sentiment. A national petition campaign sparked by newspaper editors in 1828–29 spread over the Northern states and elicited a large number from some border slave states as well. Even in the District of Columbia inhabitants filed a huge appeal to abolish slavery there. William Lloyd Garrison, in his capacity as editor of the Bennington, Vermont, *Journal of the Times*, mailed a form petition to the state's postmasters. Forty-one of them returned lists of signatures.[3] In the face of this appeal the House of Representatives was forced to take notice, even if negatively, by adopting a committee report labeling District emancipation inexpedient. But that was not the end of the matter. The flood of petitions in the 1830s stirred up both Southern tempers and Northern opposition. Senator John C. Calhoun acknowledged that by 1835 he and his colleagues faced more than the usual trickle of Quaker memorials that had come "singly and far apart." They now came in great numbers from "soured and agitated communities." Obviously, presentation of the petitions in Congress embarrassed Calhoun and other slave state senators, who were quick to label them instruments of a Northern conspiracy. Senate debate over a motion to refuse acceptance of the petitions lasted for weeks, failed of passage, and, in the end, provided invaluable exposure of the abolitionists' ideas and objectives. In the House, however, a motion quashing abolitionist petitions was successful. On May 26, 1836, the gag rule proposed by Pinckney of South Carolina was adopted. Thereafter antislavery petitions, resolutions, memorials, propositions, or papers had to be tabled, without printing or referral to committee, and could not be acted upon.[4]

The effect of this ban was quite the opposite of what its supporters intended to achieve. Slavery and the suppression of the right to petition became linked as twin natural evils in abolitionist propaganda. As they witnessed the results of the gag rule, the waves of anti-abolitionist violence, and Post Office suppression of antislavery newspapers, the supposedly neutral Northerners were aroused to defend freedom of speech, press, and the right of petition. Support for abolition became a by-product of concerns over civil liberties, and abolitionists gathered greater numbers of petitions to deluge Congress and state legislatures.

In direct response to the gag rule the American Anti-Slavery Society organized petitioning on a national basis. Under the direction of John G. Whittier, Theodore Weld, and Henry B. Stanton, printed petitions were distributed through the network of state and local societies, and later returned to the national headquarters to be conveyed to state and federal legislatures. Some 412,000 petitions were sent to the House and about 270,000 to the Senate in the 1837–38 drive. Stanton estimated that the following year the Society gathered about two million signatures.[5] In one recent reappraisal, Gerda Lerner found that women played the leading role in the 1837–38 petition campaign: females outnumbered males two to one in a sampling of 67,000 signatures on 402 petitions.[6] Another source disclosed that Massachusetts women distinguished themselves by turning in 21,000 names on a 1836–37 petition for abolishing slavery in the District of Columbia, while 9,112 names appeared on male-only petitions.[7] The general advance of the petition campaigns from 1836 to 1840 is reflected in the average number of signatures per petition:[8]

Year	Average number of signatures per petition
1836–37	32
1837–38	59
1838–39	91
1839–40	107

The seriousness of the organized petition campaign was underscored first of all by its adamant denunciation by Southern spokesmen, and second by the annual renewal of the gag rule, which was not rescinded until 1844. But other signs of the tactic's significance are the methods and the breadth of its execution. Instructions from the campaign's directors told circulators to take the appeals   wherever signers can be got. The Sandwich, New Hampshire, circulators demonstrated one successful method by going through the town from home to home. In addition, names were to be secured by following "the farmer to his field, the wood-chopper to the forest." The instructions continued: "Hail the shop keeper from his counter; call the clerk from his desk; stop the waggoner with his team; forget not the matron, ask for her daughter. Let no frown deter, no repulse baffle. Explain, discuss, argue, persuade."[9]

Not all of the signers added their names in automatic response. Many men and women did need to be persuaded by serious discussion. Abolitionists like Francis Jackson, president of the Massachusetts Anti-Slavery Society, regarded the act of signing as adding "strength and clearness . . . to the conviction of thousands."

Merton Dillon, historian of the antislavery movement, believes that "the mere act of signing one's name to an antislavery petition meant a personal commitment and identification with the movement." The difficulties in turning the tide of public opinion are noted by a correspondent in a letter to the Providence *Journal*. "Candor" (the writer's pseudonym) wrote that "the abolitionists . . . present their paper to many who are not with them on other points, but who believe that Congress has the power [to abolish slavery] and think it ought to be exercised." Protesting hostility toward the abolitionists, "Candor" continued, "Why hold up the names of some of the first men among us to reproach, merely because they have the magnanimity to *say* what we all think and feel, if we think and feel at all—viz: that slavery is a terrible evil, and we pray God and pray men to abolish it as speedily as possible."[10]

The "reproach" that "Candor" resented was widespread. One of its manifestations was physical violence. Otherwise it was seen in the fears of racial amalgamation that ran through the ranks of Northern colonizationists and conservatives. James Watson Webb, editor of the New York *Courier and Enquirer* and a vehement anti-abolitionist, urged crushing the "amalgamists." He was infected with nativistic fears that the traditional values as he knew them might be lost in any assimilation of "inferior" breeds such as the Irish and the Latin Americans into American society. Less strident anti-abolitionism was expressed by the Oneida County, New York, grand jury that condemned the 1836 petitions as "dangerous nuisances." Jacksonian politicians such as Democratic Congressman Ely Moore of New York, and Isaac Hill, boss of New Hampshire's Democratic party, constructed a theory that the "Federalists," or Whigs, were plotting to exploit the abolitionist movement against them. This was yet another variant of the conspiracy theories rife in those days. Moore argued that the targets of abolitionist petitions were Democrats and Whig workingmen.[11]

Despite these conspiratorial speculations, white workingmen and others soon helped to swell the petition and antislavery constituency. Francis Jackson believed that the agitation over the gag rule, for example, had spread the abolitionist message "into every village."[12]

William Ellery Channing, the genteel Unitarian minister of Boston's conservative Federal Street Church, had to look outside church ranks for support in his slowly maturing commitment to radical abolitionism. According to his biographer, Channing came to believe that "the harvest of Abolitionism" would be reaped by the "farmers, mechanics, and other working men" who already appeared to have been well represented in the movement. But he had earlier complained that abolitionists appealed indiscriminately to "young and old, pupils from schools, females hardly arrived at years of discretion, the ignorant, the excitable, the impetuous," and even "preached their doctrine to the colored people, and collected these into their societies." The distance that many Unitarian ministers tried to place between themselves and the abolitionist movement reflected their upper-class character and predilections. But they also hinted at the social qualities of the abolitionist constituency. In their eyes, abolitionists—with the exception of the "aristocratic demagogue" Wendell Phillips—were "poor, humble, despised people, of no influence; men one could not ask to dine."[13] (Shades of the aristocratic planter class who set the tone and dominated the Southern plantation!) The haughty Unitarian statement ignored the hundreds of men and women in the movement whom one met in the "best" parlors and church vestibules and in the academic halls and lyceums across the country. These influential, educated, articulate, even wealthy people were in the middle and upper classes of society. The cream of their crop, in the Boston-Cambridge establishment, proved resilient and responsive to the antislavery appeal. They were not attracted to the movement because of supposed fears over loss of status.[14] Serene and self-confident, they nonetheless reacted with some alarm at slavery's disturbance of republican virtues. But they failed to link the offenses of industrialism to the offensive slave system, as workingmen's spokesmen did.

As for those the ministers "would not ask to dine," presumably those in the laboring classes, data in this book affirm that they too were well represented in the antislavery constituency and shared upper-class concerns over the flawed republic.

NOTES

1. The petitions used in this study are in the National Archives, Record Group 233 (for the House of Representatives), Legislative Records, Civil Archives Division, Washington, D.C. These are designated by an "HR" number, e.g., HR24 stands for the 24th Con-

gress, House of Representatives. "Library of Congress Collection" and a Box number stand for petitions also stored in RG233.

Petitions of the 1830s:

For abolition of slavery in the District of Columbia

Lynn, March 21, 1836—HR24A–G22.4

      January 3, 1838—Library of Congress Collection, Box 99

      December 18, 1838—HR25A–H1.8

Fall River, February 18, 1839—HR25A–H1.8 (LC Coll., Box 134)

Worcester, December 20, 1838—HR25A (LC Coll., Box 122)

Utica, March 21, 1836—HR24A–G.22.4

      September 26, 1837—HR25A–H1.8

Rome, (September-December) 1837—HR25A–H1.8

Schenectady, 1838—HR25A–H1.8

Lowell, June 6, 1836—HR24A–G22.4

Against the gag rule

Lynn, March 12, 1838—LC Coll., Box 100

Fall River, February 18, 1839—HR25A–H1.7 (LC Coll., Box 134)

Harvard, February 18, 1839—LC Coll., Box 131

Northborough, February 18, 1839—LC Coll., Box 131

Springfield, February 14, 1838—HR25A–File 627, Bundle 12

Against annexation of Texas

Lynn, September 19, 1837—HR25A–H1.1

Fall River, March 12, 1838—HR25A–H1.1

Utica, September 19, 1837—HR25A–H1.1

Petitions against the Kansas-Nebraska Act and/or Repeal of the Missouri Compromise:

Utica, Rome, and New Hartford petitions were part of an Oneida County, New York, petition of more than 4,000 signers in many of its towns—HR33A–G24.2

Schenectady, March 20, 1854—HR33A–G24.4 (LC Coll., Box 153)

Ogdensburgh, March 29, and February 24, 1854—HR33A–G24.2 "Call for County Convention," signed by "Electors and Residents" of Oswegatchie Township, St. Lawrence County, New York—Ogdensburgh *Sentinel*, August 1, 1854.

Fall River, March 13, 1854—HR33A

Lynn, July 26, 1854—HR33A–G10.10

Springfield, undated—HR33A–G24.2

Worcester, February 12 and 17, 1855, to United States Senate, in Record Group 46, 33d Cong., 2d sess.

   2. Russel B. Nye, *Fettered Freedom: Civil Liberties and The Slavery Controversy, 1830-1860* (East Lansing: Michigan State College Press, 1949), p. 37.

3. Gilbert Hobbs Barnes, *The Antislavery Impulse, 1830-1844* (Washington: American Historical Association, 1933), pp. 109, 253.

4. Ibid., pp. 110, 131–33; Nye, *Fettered Freedom*, pp. 36–37.

5. *The Liberator*, September 21, 1838.

6. Gerda Lerner, *The Majority Finds Its Past* (New York: Oxford University Press, 1980), pp. 112–28.

7. *The Liberator*, April 23, 1837; Ellen Henle suggests that the lower male participation in Sandwich, New Hampshire, may have been due to the absence of many men who had migrated to western New York and Ohio. See Henle, "'Forget Not the Matron': Sandwich Women and Antislavery in the Antebellum Years," *Fifty–Ninth Annual Excursion of the Sandwich Historical Society*, August 27, 1978, p. 34.

8. Barnes, *Antislavery Impulse*, p. 266.

9. Ibid., p. 136; Henle, "'Forget Not the Matron'," p. 33; Patricia Heard, "'One Blood All Nations': Antislavery Petitions in Sandwich," in *Fifty–Ninth Annual Excursion*, p. 30.

10. Jane H. and William H. Pease, *The Antislavery Argument* (Indianapolis: Bobbs-Merrill, 1965), p. 398; Merton L. Dillon, *The Abolitionists: The Growth of A Dissenting Minority* (DeKalb: Northern Illinois University Press, 1974), p. 102; *The Providence Journal*, February 18, 1837.

11. Leonard L. Richards, *Gentlemen of Property and Standing: Anti-Abolition Mobs in Jacksonian America* (New York: Oxford University Press, 1970), pp. 31–32; James L. Crouthamel, *James Watson Webb: A Biography* (Middletown, Conn.: Wesleyan University Press, 1969), pp. 54–56; Nye, *Fettered Freedom*, p. 48; George Stevens, *New York Typographical Union No. 6: Study of a Modern Trade Union and its Predecessors* (Albany: J. B. Lyon, 1913), p. 189; Donald B. Cole, *Jacksonian Democracy in New Hampshire, 1800-1851* (Cambridge: Harvard University Press, 1970), p. 176.

12. Pease and Pease, *Antislavery Argument*, p. 401.

13. Octavius B. Frothingham, *Boston Unitarianism, 1820-1850* (New York, 1890), cited by Daniel Walker Howe, *The Unitarian Conscience: Harvard Moral Philosophy, 1805-1861* (Cambridge: Harvard University Press, 1970), p. 176; Channing, *Works*, vol. 2, p. 128; Jack Mendelsohn, *William Ellery Channing: The Reluctant Radical* (Boston: Little, Brown, 1971), pp. 258–59.

14. Donald, "Toward a Reconsideration of Abolitionists," pp. 33–34.

CHAPTER 6

The 1830s Antislavery Constituency: Social Profile

The people who signed antislavery petitions made up a grand coalition of social groups for reform. The men and women in the antislavery campaign lived in all parts of the cities and in their nearby countrysides. They came from all walks of life. Their varied occupations, from "agent" to "wool grader," were listed under at least 120 out of a possible 212 classifications used in this study. They varied in age from eighteen years to eighty. Most were born in the states in which they lived at the time of signing; some were born in neighboring states. The large number of petitioners who could not be found suggests the marked transiency of the American people. The overwhelming portion of the petitioners—from 60 to 70 percent—owned no real estate. If they did own property, it tended to be real estate assessed at between $1,000 and $5,000. Seventy percent of the petitioners owned no personal property of assessable value. Those who did have taxable possessions tended to fall in the low bracket of $101 to $500.

Those of the signers who were church members were, with one exception, Protestants. Eleven denominations are represented in this study, although only four of them claim more than 15 percent each of the total signers in the sampling. The better represented denominations were Baptist, Methodist,

Presbyterian, and Congregationalist. These church identifications must be regarded with some qualification. On the one hand many men chose to remain outside of formal church membership. Since no one had reason to list these "nothingarians," it is not possible to judge their numbers. On the other hand, many otherwise religious men tended to leave church membership to the women in their families, which points to the "feminization" of American religion. In addition, there is some distortion of the petitioners' denominational identities because many church membership lists could not be found in the cities under study.[1] Our data provide an aggregate of church membership for only 28 percent of the 1,633 men in the petition sample for the 1830s.

The attributes of the signers, taken together, make for a statistical picture of the antislavery social base. Each of the variables describing them—birthplace, age, property, occupation, religious affiliation, and political tendency in the special cases of Harvard and Northborough men—bears further comment. The first five are discussed in this chapter; politics in chapter 7.

The shared republican heritage of the petitioners is suggested by their national and regional origins. Ninety-five percent of the 925 petitioners were native-born Americans. Seventy percent were born in Massachusetts, and about 19 percent claimed the other New England states as birthplaces (see Table 6–1). New York is represented by a little under 5 percent. The Bay State's lopsided domination of these statistics reflects its cities' larger representation in the study. But the Massachusetts figures here suggest the well-known migration that was a feature of Western nations' industrialization in general and of the United States distinctively. As an example, one-third of Utica's petitioners were born in New York State but another 25 percent were born in New England states. Foreign-born petitioners comprised only 5.5 percent of the total. All were from English-speaking countries. Twenty-one men born in England were followed by 11 from Ireland, 10 from Wales, 7 from Scotland, and 1 from Canada.

The ages of the petitioners were derived from the 1850 census (see Table 6–2; the appropriate subtraction of years was

Table 6–1
Birthplaces of 1830s Petitioners

STATE OR NATION	(N)	%
New York	46	4.9
Maine	19	2.1
Vermont	8	.9
New Hampshire	55	5.9
Massachusetts	653	70.6
Connecticut	36	3.9
Rhode Island	55	5.9
Other States	2	.2
England	21	2.3
Scotland	7	.8
Ireland	11	1.2
Wales	10	1.1
Canada	1	.1
Other Countries	1	.1
Total	925	100

Table 6–2
Age of 1830s Petitioners

AGE GROUP	(N)	%
Under 18 years	18	2.0
19 to 29	336	36.5
30 to 39	277	30.0
40 to 49	187	20.3
50 to 59	79	8.6
60 and older	24	2.6
Total	921	100

made to determine their age at the time of signing). The largest portion of the signers included men from 19 to 39 years. Their average age was 35.5 years. This is three years older than the average age of all males in the census for these places. This small age gap does not alter their place in the largest male age group of the population.

The figures show that the petitioners, as members of this age group, tended to be the most mobile, least propertied, and most economically expectant in the population. Economic change was sending large numbers into the cities to find employment. Boom times promoted geographical mobility and encouraged optimism among entrepreneurial types as well as among wage earners. Men in all walks of life, from laborers and clerks to skilled journeymen and shopkeepers, looked toward the day when they would enjoy economic independence, prestige and respectable social standing, and a dignified old age. While an independent farm homestead became the goal of many, inexorable forces turned the search into a process of urbanization instead. And for many such men their "failures" in this regard seem to have soured the new flavors of republicanism. Blacks especially felt this letdown.

Men came to the cities to seek work and to participate in the "restless pursuit of wealth," but the 1830s were marked by disturbing struggles by men and women merely to defend their working conditions and living standards. Among the masses of propertyless city dwellers the rhetoric of egalitarianism might understandably have been taken as buncombe. In every age group in the manufacturing cities of this study, but especially among the 19 to 39 year olds, large percentages were not property owners. If they owned any property, the petitioners were more likely to be young skilled men among the working classes, or merchants or professionals among the middle classes (see Tables 6–3 and 6–4). Their holdings became more valuable as they grew older and more established in their trades and in their businesses. Men in the $1,001 to

Table 6–3
1830s Petitioners' Occupation Groups by Age Groups
(In Percentages)

Occupational Group	Age Groups			
	19–29	30–39	40–49	50–59
1. Unskilled	6.9	4.5	8.1	4.3
2. Semiskilled	3.1	2.6	1.0	4.3
3. Proprietor–Manager–Official	20.0	32.7	24.2	12.8
4. Skilled	53.1	42.3	39.4	42.6
5. Commerce & Sales	5.6	4.5	3.0	0
6. Semi-Professional	0	1.9	0	2.1
7. Professional	4.4	1.3	7.1	10.6
8. Farmers	6.3	10.3	16.2	23.4

Table 6–4
1830s Petitioners' Assessed Real Estate by Age Groups
(In Percentages)

Real Estate Valued at	Age Groups			
	19–29	30–39	40–49	50–59
None	81.0	66.2	55.7	21.0
Less than $200	1.5	2.2	0	0
$201–$500	10.6	22.3	21.1	25.0
$501–$1,000	2.3	5.8	2.6	0
$1,001–$5,000	2.3	2.9	12.5	18.4
$5,001–$10,000	1.5	.7	1.1	2.6
More than $10,000	.8	0	1.1	0

$5,000 range were more numerous among the 40 to 60 year olds. But those in the lower property category, $1,000 and less, clustered in that younger group, from 19 to 39 years old. This age-property relationship is not surprising; as Robert Doherty found, it appeared in large and small Massachusetts towns.[2] It does remind us that the restless and ambitious younger men, and the hard-pressed and dissatisfied workingmen, shared a concern about the quality and future of their democratic society and culture. Further consideration of petitioners' property values will follow below. But first we consider the constituency's occupational structure.

As many historians and social theorists have discovered in the last 190 years or so, defining social class has become a nettlesome intellectual exercise. The best that most social scientists and historians appear able to do is to admit that occupation is at least pro tempore the best single indicator of class. Without entering into the important and complex discussion of the flaws and shortcomings of such an apparently simple and economist definition of class, I have chosen to regard occupation as a decisive ingredient in defining social class as a relationship of the mode of production (emergent industrial capitalism), and as a relationship to the means of production and the ownership of property. Even if we adopt Edward Thompson's modern classical redefinition of class as "a happening," it is plain that class is a variable *and* a fixed category in the social structure of modern society. It appears to have been carving out that place for itself in life and in theoretical discussions with the birth of industrial capitalism, in the late eighteenth and through the next two centuries.[3]

An occupational analysis of 1,530 petitioners in seven cities demonstrates the social and economic class base of the constituency. The organization of the world of work utilized here is an adaptation of one used by Peter Knights for his quantitative analysis of Boston's antebellum population.[4] It reflects the early period of industrialization. The large proportion of artisans in the structure suggests the preponderance of relatively small manufactories and mills. In order to provide some base of comparison with the whole body of petitioners, Table 6–5 also presents the occupational structure of all males over 15 years of age in Utica, Schenectady and Lynn.

Utica's structure may well be the most valuable inasmuch as the changes occurring there in the mid-1830s fall between the more industrially advanced Fall River, Lynn, and Worcester and the less advanced Rome and Schenectady. Consideration must also be given to Lynn's overwhelming number of cordwainers, which tends to enlarge the artisan group beyond its share in other towns. Schenectady's skilled group of 294 men was a diverse one including carpenters, masons, blacksmiths, shoemakers, machinists, and tailors. Utica's skilled population of 805 men offered a larger range of occupations including coopers, locksmiths, stonecutters, tinsmiths, moulders, and printers in addition to the others in Schenectady.

Table 6–5
Occupations of Petitioners and Members of Antislavery Societies (Percentages)

Occupational Group	Petitioners in Seven Cities (N=1530)	Society Members	Male Occupational Group Structure in the Total Population of Three Cities			
			Utica (1837)	Schenectady (1841)	Lynn, Mass. (1832)	(1841)
1. Unskilled & Menial Service	4.0	1.1	13.2	2.7	1.7	1.3
2. Semi-skilled & Service	2.5	2.3	5.3	.9	5.5	6.5
3. Proprietor-Manager-Official	22.5	18.4	19.2	25.0	13.0	17.3
4. Skilled	53.8	64.4	42.6	52.3	72.8	66.8
5. Commerce & Sales	4.1	3.4	10.3	4.4	.5	1.3
6. Semi-Professional	.7	1.1	.7	.7		
7. Professional	4.8	1.1	5.2	12.6	2.1	2.6
8. Farmers	6.3	4.6	1.5	.5	4.2	4.1
9. Miscellaneous	1.5	3.4	1.9	.5		

Moreover, Utica's occupational structure is the most immediately contemporaneous with the antislavery petition activity, being compiled from 1837–38 city directory listings.[5]

Skilled men in occupations involving distinctive local industry specialization are more numerous than other craftsmen among the signers. The Lynn cordwainers employed by local shoe manufacturers, Springfield armorers probably employed at the federal arsenal, Worcester machinists in the wire and tool and machinery-making shops, and Utica's numerous tailors all contributed significant proportions of artisan antislavery petitioners.

Table 6–6
Percentage of Skilled Men among 1830s Petitioners

	%	N
Fall River	43.5	111
Lynn	67.8	301
Springfield	42.3	63
Worcester	49.2	87
Rome	41.2	7
Schenectady	61.3	38
Utica	40.1	130

That these men comprise a majority of the petitioners may be due in part to two distortions. One is created by the very large percentage of cordwainers in Lynn, and by Schenectady's small shop structure which permitted artisans to dominate a small sample. The search among Schenectady's petitioners, for example, failed to turn up signers in the commerce and sales (5), semiprofessional (6), and farmer (8) categories. Skilled men represented between 40 and 67 percent of the petitioners in the cities under study (see Table 6–6).

Our inability to separate master craftsmen/employers from

wage-earning journeymen may also tend to enlarge the skilled group unrealistically. Some skilled men should be considered proprietors or manufacturers in category 3. If the 53.8 percent of all the petitioners who were skilled were to be divided between employer and employed, in a ratio approximately four to one, as in Jeffersonian preindustrial times, the wage-earning skilled men would amount to about 43 percent of the petitioners.[6] This would put them directly parallel to the Utica artisans' share of the working population. Perhaps this would reflect a more representative proportion of skilled men among signers. They would also resemble New York City workingmen, whose share of antislavery petitions signatures between 1835 and 1839 ranged from 32 percent to 47 percent, with four of the memorials containing 41 percent artisans or more.[7]

Working-class women, although nonvoters, contributed to the immense antislavery endeavor. Most of them were operatives—weavers, spinners, dyers, and others—in woolen and cotton mills. Some were "sewing girls" in merchant tailor shops. We should expect to find strong antislavery support among the women factory workers in Fall River, Worcester, Springfield, and Lynn. But it is Lowell where data are available to identify women petitioners, especially the mill workers among 1,409 signers of an 1836 petition.

Like the workingmen in our petition population, the women signers held the "more skilled" jobs at the Hamilton Manufacturing Company and outnumbered the "least skilled."[8] A sample of 894 names yielded 229 that were linked to jobs in eight Lowell textile companies, four that held non-mill occupations, and nine that resided in company boarding houses but whose occupations are unknown. The class and condition of 650 women not identified with the Lowell factories remain unknown as well. However, the 242 whose working-class identities are known represent 16.8 percent of those who signed the petition. This is significant evidence of working-class participation in the antislavery movement.

Sixty-three workers employed in the Hamilton Company factory were among the sampled 242. This was the largest representation among the Lowell companies' workers. Fifty signers worked at the Merrimac works; 34 at Lawrence Manufacturing Company; and 21 at the Appleton Mills. Smaller numbers of signers were employed at the Boott, Middlesex, Suffolk, and Tremont mills. Of the Hamilton works signers, 35, or 67.3 percent, whose job titles are known, worked at "more skilled" occupations. Twenty-two were weavers, 1 was a dresser, 3 were drawing-in hands, and 9 were warpers. All but the dresser were overrepresentative of their classifications (compared with their share of the general occupational structure) in the factory, where a total of 881 females were employed in July 1836 (see Table 6–7).

Table 6–7
Women Petitioners at Hamilton Manufacturing Company, 1836

Occupation	N	% of petitioners at Hamilton	% of Hamilton employees (N=881) in job title
"more skilled"			
Weaver	22	42.0	35.9
Dresser	1	1.9	4.3
Warper	9	17.3	2.6
Drawing-in Hand	3	5.8	3.0
Total	35	67.3	45.8
"least skilled"			
Sparehand	5	9.6	21.0
Drawer	2	3.8	6.8
Spinner	0		15.2
Speeder	2]		[
Filling	4]	19.2	[6.2*
"Worker"	4]		[
Total	17	32.6	
Unknown	11		
Total	63		

*Described as "minor jobs."

The female workers were among the first generation of a new social group: factory workers dependent on wages received for the sale of their labor power. Moderately well-off New Hampshire and Massachusetts farm families were the principal source from which the new industrialists obtained that valuable commodity. Usually, the women who came to work sought independence, not relief from poverty or economic pressure. They brought with them much more than economic values. These were the proud and self-conscious descendants of the men and women who had made the American Revolution. Most of them, including the 229 mill workers in our sample, lived in boarding houses. Thomas Dublin shows that these residences became a critical element in the shaping of the working women's community. In its cultural and social milieu the women became actively concerned not only with their own working conditions but with those of the distant black slaves. These young women were highly conscious of their heritage and were not shy in advancing their case against wage cuts and company rent increases, over which they went on strike in 1834 and in 1836. Their strike proclamation stated, "And as we are free, we would remain in possession of what kind Providence has bestowed upon us, and remain daughters of freemen still." They linked wage cutting to the manufacturers' "general plan" to reduce them to "slaves." Their hostility stemmed from resentment over their neighbors' perception of them as "factory slaves," a derogatory designation such as that heaped on Southern mill town workers decades later— "lintheads." Putting their names on antislavery petitions represented only another way of declaring their overdue independence. These working-class signers thus asserted their rights as workers and as women virtually at the same time that they joined a protest against enslavement of black laborers.

In the industrial revolution slavery was perceived to be the negation of the free labor system's objectives. For workers, slavery was not only an evil and iniquity offensive to religion and political and social philosophy. It was a present reality slightly modified by the payment of wages but nonetheless slavery insofar as it robbed the factory operative and the artisan of independence in the workplace. "Wage slavery" was considered as diminishing the dignity of labor and self-governance in a basic sphere of living. Workers gave voice to those resentments and concerns.

The marching song of the 1836 Lowell strikers contained these lines:

> Oh, isn't it a pity, such a pretty girl as I—
> Should be sent to the factory to pine away and die?
> Oh! I cannot be a slave
> For I'm so fond of liberty
> That I cannot be a slave.

At Woonsocket, a picture of factory village relations in 1833 was projected in a lengthy series of rhymes, of which these lines are a small part:

> For liberty our fathers fought
> Which with their blood, they dearly bought,
> The Fac'try system sets at naught.
> A slave at morn, a slave at eve,
> It doth my inmost feelings grieve.

When the workers of the Cocheco Company at Dover, New Hampshire, turned out in 1834 against a wage cut, their resolutions included this protest: "However freely the epithet of 'factory slave' may be bestowed upon us, we will never deserve it by a base and cringing submission to proud wealth or haughty insolence." Here was American republicanism refracted through the prism of working class consciousness, a vivid illumination of class feeling among working women and men.

Eleven years later, it was estimated that if the Lowell women who signed a petition against the extension of slavery "were to join hand in hand" they could reach more than a mile. The newspaper reporting this in 1845 noted that "probably not a few of them [the signers] are the young women, called 'white slaves' at the South, who work in the factories."[9]

Only a tiny fraction of the male petitioners were unskilled laborers. In all seven cities there were only fifty-nine. However, twenty-seven of them were from Fall River. The sources do not tell us more than their occupational titles, but it is tempting to believe that they might have been employed in the rows of stone factory buildings spreading along the Quequechan River, or "The Stream," between the Taunton River and Watuppa Pond. Taken together with other men in the lowest two groups, they make up only 6.5 percent of the petitioners. Measured against our standard, the total number of unskilled and semiskilled, they are seriously underrepresented. Their presence, however, augments the artisan group in bringing into prominence the working-class component in the antislavery constituency.

The predominance of artisans and working-class petitioners does not deny, entirely, the leading role in abolitionism that historians have assigned to the middle class. Representatives of that class are included in four, and possibly five, of the groups that I have identified in occupational terms. These are the proprietors, managers, and officials (3), which includes merchants, manufacturers, traders, owners of shops, inns, hotels, boarding houses, dealers in lumber and supplies, peddlers, livery stable owners, postmasters, judges, customs officers, and the like; commercial and sales (5), which includes clerks, auctioneers, agents, accountants, and bank tellers and cashiers; semiprofessionals (6), including dentists, architects, draftsmen, artists, evangelists and missionaries, and oculists; professionals (7), physicians, lawyers, teachers, civil engineers, clergymen, editors, and druggists; and probably some of the property-owning (means of production in manufacturing) members of the skilled (4) group.

The apparent overrepresentation of group 3 among the petitioners underscores the role played by rising manufacturers, merchants, and some local political figures in the reform movement. Men involved in advancing the newest aspects of business and industry were also activists in liberal social reform movements, temperance, and abolitionism. Together with the professionals and commerce-and-sales men, they tended to own more and more of the economy and to dominate society, government and institutions. Their fundamental interest in a free-enterprise economy, based on free labor, led them into a strategic if temporary coalition with other middle-class groups and skilled artisans.

A more thorough examination of property values reveals further evidence of social class standings in the antislavery constituency. Although these data may be an imprecise and static measure of mere economic condition, they do offer an indication of both social class and individual life styles and circumstances.

The bulk of the petitioners held no assessable real estate (see Table 6–8). Of the 1,225 men for whom municipal tax books were available, 60 percent, or 743, were propertyless. Of the property owners, the large number of very modest holdings, in the range of $201 to $500, reveals the far from affluent nature of the petitioners. Some men of great wealth, with property worth upwards of ten, twenty, or thirty thousand dollars, were among the signers. In each of the larger cities, at least one prosperous manufacturer or leading merchant could be found. Such men appear in the statistics as a small percentage of the signers.

The antislavery men as a body owned less than their fellow citizens. Thus, for example, the mean real estate value of Lynn taxpayers in 1837 is estimated at $435 to $502, but the mean value of all Lynn male petitioners' property was approximately $300. If only the property holders are compared, the gap widens. City of Lynn property owners' mean values were appoximately $487. In Utica, similar distinctions appear. The mean value of Utica property owners' real estate in 1835 was $1,023 (see Table 6–9). The mean property value of all of the Utica petitioners fell to $336. The average for all 1,225 petitioners for whom data are available is $356 (from Table 6–8). Finally, using City of Lynn tax records, a comparison shows 95 percent of the petitioners falling below the $1,000 mark while 85 percent of all Lynn polls were in that range of real property values.

The economic standings of the petitioners is made even more vivid in a cross-tabulation of their real estate values with occupational groups. As Table 6–10 illustrates, every one of the groups had some propertyless members. But the very high

Table 6–8
Assessed Value of Petitioners' Real Property, 1830s

Amount Owned	(N)	%	Antislavery Society members (Lynn & Worcester)		Utica leaders in 1835	
			(N)	%	(N)	%
None	743	60.7	53	36.1	46	56.1
Less than $200	53	4.3	10	6.8		
$201 to $500	272	22.2	44	29.9	17	20.7
$501 to $1,000	91	7.4	25	17.0	11	13.4
$1,001 to $5,000	50	4.1	10	6.8	4	4.9
$5,001 to $10,000	10	.8	3	2.0	4	4.9
More than $10,000	6	.5	2	1.4		
Total	1225	100	147	100	82	100

Average value of all petitioners = $356
Average value of property owners = $906

Table 6–9
Average Value of Petitioners' Real Estate by Cities

City	Average value of signers on tax rolls		Average of Signers with property		Average of men on tax rolls of Utica (1835) and Lynn (1837)	
	(N)	Value	(N)	Value	(N)	Value
Utica	313	$336	103	$1,023	760	$3,495
Fall River			68	$1,225		
Lynn	383	$300	236	$ 487		$1,050
Worcester	235	$959	75	$1,287		

Table 6–10
Assessed Value of 1830s Petitioners' Real Property by Their Occupational Groups

Amount	1. Unskilled	2. Semi-skilled	3. Propr.-Mgr.-Official	4. Skilled	5. Comm. & Sales
None	40	11	129	353	34
Less than $200	1	1	11	35	3
$201 to $500	7	5	60	159	8
$501 to $1,000		1	28	41	3
$1,001 to $5,000			23	12	1
$5,001 to $10,000			4	4	
More than $10,000			3	1	
Totals	48	18	258	605	49
%	4.2	1.6	22.7	53.3	4.3

proportions of nonownership or very modestly valued property among the skilled men suggests an overwhelmingly wage-earner rather than a proprietor class. Almost 60 percent of the skilled would appear to be boarders or renters, and 26 percent owned simply domiciles assessed at between $201 and $500. The professionals along with the semiprofessionals enjoyed prestige and community respect frequently denied to the lowly mechanic, but they appear to have been even poorer than the skilled men. Poorer still were the unskilled and semi-skilled, as we should expect. Those at the upper end of the property scale were proprietors, managers and officials. They owned significant real estate, valued from $1,000 to well over $10,000.[10] In Lynn, only 6 percent of all taxpayers were in the higher bracket of $2,000 or more. An even smaller percentage of the 497 petitioners fell in the $5,000-and-higher category: a mere 1.3 percent. The few petitioners at those levels of wealth appeared to be self-made manufacturers and entrepreneurs for the most part.

Personal property assessments, too, reinforce the image of an antislavery constituency comprised primarily of men of modest means. A characteristic which the petitioners shared with members of abolition societies was that very large numbers were propertyless from the assessors' viewpoint. Few owned domestic animals, buggies or carriages, or the tools and raw materials of their trades. Some did have these necessary items of independent artisan production and status. Some also had other taxable income which fell into the personal property category, such as interest, dividends, and stock in trade or bank savings deposits. But 70 percent of the petitioners owned none of these (see Table 6–11).

The differing material conditions may be appreciated in a few examples chosen at random. At one level of the property hierarchy were the Fall River baker, King L. Runnels, who was taxed on $1,000 of real estate and $1,350 of personal property, and David Anthony, president of the Fall River Bank and deacon of the First Congregational Church, who was taxed on real estate valued at $10,200. At lower economic levels were such men as Edward P. Buffinton with no taxable real estate and $300 of personal property and Richard Chatburn, an En-

Table 6–11
Value of 1830s Petitioners' Personal Property

Amount	(N)	%
None	553	70.3
Less than $100	41	5.2
$101 to $500	87	11.1
$501 to $1,000	41	5.2
$1,001 to $5,000	56	7.1
$5,001 to $10,000+	9	1.1
Total	787	100

Average value all signers = $335.58
Average value signer/property owners = $1,128

glish-born engraver with no taxable real estate and no mention of personal property in the 1838 assessor's book of Fall River. In the same status in that city were such men as Shubael Pease, cabinetmaker; Perry M. Peckham, planemaker; and James Ramsbotham, a laborer born in England. In 1840 Baxter Barnes, a Worcester carpenter, was taxed on real estate assessed at $1,000 and personal property assessed at "none"; the wire factory worker Absalom Bellows was taxed on personal items worth only $400, but in that same year William Dickinson, cashier of the Worcester Central Bank, was taxed on $800 of real estate and $500 in personal property. The grocery proprietor Edmund F. Dixie owned $5,850 of real estate and was also taxed on $6,000 of stock in his business; Edward Earle, Quaker iron dealer and officer of the antislavery society, owned $7,000 in real estate and $1,000 in bank stock, and his company was assessed for $5,000 of real estate and $7,000 "stock in business." His relative, John Milton Earle, editor and publisher of *The Spy*, one of New England's oldest newspapers, held real estate worth $3,800 and personal property of $3,000, which was the newspaper establishment. But near the top of the affluent group was one of Worcester's most prosperous and civic-minded industrial capitalists, William B. Fox. In 1840 his company's factories and buildings were worth $13,000, his own real estate $4,000, personal items $150, and his company's machinery and stock (for sash and blind manufacture) $8,000. The wealthy builder Alpheus Merrifield, listed as a carpenter in the 1844 city directory and the 1850 census, was worth over $50,000 in 1840. William T. Merrifield, also a sash and blind maker, and listed as a carpenter, declared his real estate to be worth $80,000 in 1850. Yet not far away from him lived the wire factory machinist Rufus W. Newton, with "none" listed for both real and personal property. Between those extremes could be found a body of men with ostensibly divergent interests and stakes in the socioeconomic system, yet apparently united in calling for the abolition of slavery.

Although their tax obligations seemed small or non-existent, the men without assessable property were not impoverished. They were men of small means, smaller than their peers'. The mean personal property assessment of the 787 petitioners found in the tax records was $335.58, and of the 234 who actually were assessed for their property, the mean was $1,128 (see Tables 6–11 and 6–12). This is less than half that of the 103 Utica petitioners who owned property in 1835— $3,621.

The bulk of the propertied petitioners are in a middle economic level. The middle-class men—merchants, manufacturers, proprietors, managers, and officials—clustered in the $1,001 to $5,000 category of personal property ownership. Professionals and semiprofessionals tended to be in the same range. Artisans slipped below them by as much as four to five thousand dollars in some cases and by only a few dollars in others. Almost 11 percent of the skilled men owned from $101 to $500 of personal property (see Table 6–13).

All of the indicators of economic inequality described by the data help to delineate social classes. In both the total population and the antislavery constituency differences in occupa-

Table 6–12
Average Value of 1830s Petitioners' Personal Property by Cities

City	Signers on Tax rolls		Signers with Property	
	(N)	Value	(N)	Value
Fall River	211	$398	69	$1,218
Lynn	381	$337	131	$ 982
Worcester	235	$453	91	$1,171

tional groups and the disparities in property ownership further delineate class divisions. In addition, it is well to recall, real conflicts of class interests led the Lowell women to strike, the Lynn cordwainers to establish their journeymen's benevolent and trade union organizations, and Fall River operatives to organize their own cooperative stores.[11] Fortunately for the middle-class men and women, these workers brought a broad current of mainstream America to the common cause of abolitionism. William West, a workers' leader, had furnished the rallying slogan for the mechanics and laborers: "down with all slavery—wages and chattel."[12] On that basis employees could strike against their employers and still join them in a protest against black chattel slavery. Their action

Table 6–13
Assessed Value of 1830s Petitioners' Personal Property by Their Occupational Groups

Amount	1. Unskilled & Menial Svce.	2. Semiskilled & Service	3. Propr-Mgr-Offcl.	4. Skilled	5. Commerce & Sales
None	14	3	77	327	17
Less than $100	1	2	8	23	
$101 to $500	1		22	45	
$501 to $1,000			15	12	1
$1,001 to $5,000	1		31	9	1
$5,000 to $10,000+			6	1	
Total	17	5	159	417	19
%	2.3	.7	22.0	57.7	2.6

in this regard helps to unchain the American working class from the theory of a narrow "job consciousness."[13] Finally, these working-class petitioners help to dispel the theory that Northern white workingmen opposed abolitionism because they feared black job competition following emancipation of the slaves.

Lynn cordwainers and manufacturers provide a specific test case of the racial competition model. Paul Faler's excellent study of Lynn's industrial revolution asserted that "the mechanic . . . was hostile to slavery as an unjust system of labor, but equally hostile to blacks."[14] The first half of his statement has been reinforced by the petitioners' profile in this book. The second remains to be demonstrated, for Faler fails to support it with evidence. Now we have found data with which to test the assertion.

In January 1839, 171 angry anti-abolitionists in Lynn, unable to tolerate a women's petition for equal rights regardless of color, pilloried the signers in a counterpetition to the state legislature. The anti-abolitionist statement sardonically granted the 786 women petitioners the "privilege" "to marry, intermarry, or associate with any Negro, Indian, Hottentot, or any other being in human shape, at their will and pleasure, provided they do not in any way transgress the law over and above the petition."[15] Who were these men and how did they compare with Lynn's antislavery petitioners? Could a mechanics' group such as the cordwainers be as hostile to blacks as Faler maintains? The following data may help to find an answer to these questions.

The 171 anti-abolitionists were, like the male antislavery petitioners, in all of the occupational groups. Job titles have been found for 112 of them and they can be compared to those of 569 antislavery men (see Table 6–14). Skilled men make up the largest group in both occupational structures, with antislavery craftsmen almost 8 percent higher than their opposites. The notable feature of the anti-abolitionists is their greater percentages in the lower skill categories. This is underscored by the absence of professionals and the lagging bloc of proprietors-managers-officials. The implication that the anti-abolitionists would also be poorer is borne out by the compar-

Table 6–14
Occupational Structure of Lynn, Massachusetts, Abolitionist Petitioners and Anti-Abolitionists

Occupational Group	Lynn Abolitionist Petitioners		Lynn Anti- Abolitionists		All 1830s Abolitionist Petitioners	
	(N)	%	(N)	%	(N)	%
1. Unskilled & Menial Service	8	1.4	4	3.6	61	4.0
2. Semiskilled & Service	11	1.9	13	11.6	38	2.5
3. Propr-Mgr-Offcl	113	19.9	17	15.2	344	22.5
4. Skilled	386	67.8	68	60.7	823	53.8
5. Commerce & Sales	8	1.4	5	4.5	62	4.1
6. Semi-Prof'nl	2	.4	2	1.8	10	.7
7. Professional	12	2.1			73	4.8
8. Farmers	16	2.8	3	2.7	96	6.3
9. Miscellaneous	13	2.3			23	1.5
Total	569		112		1530	

ison of their real property assessments with those of the antislavery men. The high proportion of propertyless anti-abolitionists is impressive in itself, and important in comparison with antislavery property ownership (see Table 6–15). Racial fears could have been heightened by resentment over lower economic status, and by anxiety over a challenge to male supremacy. Such phobias could also be due to a general sense of uncertainty in parlous times, when men and machines were

Table 6–15
Assessed Value of Real Property Owned by Lynn Abolitionist Petitioners and Anti-Abolitionists

Amount	Abolitionist Petitioners (N)	%	Anti-Abolitionists (N)	%
None	147	38.4	53	60.9
Less than $200	44	11.5	2	2.3
$201 to $500	123	32.1	22	25.3
$501 to $1,000	62	16.2	10	11.5
$1,001 to $5,000	7	1.8		
Total	383	100	87	100

overturning traditions, unsettling fixed economic relations, and transforming the visible and palpable world. Racial intermarriage may have been one of the more apparent of such cultural disturbances. And sarcasm was an easy and inexpensive weapon to combat such subversion. So much might be inferred and surmised on the basis of the occupational and property data describing the opposite groups of men. Moreover, the average higher age of the anti-amalgamationists—34.3 years—as compared to the pro-abolitionists—29.7—also suggests men with fixed traditional values and goals that might be threatened by interracial marriage, or even by black male job competition. Almost 40 percent of the anti-amalgamationists were between 30 and 39 years; almost 41 percent of the antislavery petitioners were between the ages of 19 and 29.

The absolute numbers suggest another aspect of the comparison. However pointed and embittered their emphasis on the unreal intermarriage possibilities, only 171 men voiced their opposition to the petition for black equal rights, and by extension, against abolitionism. Yet they opposed a total of 786 women in this instance, almost five times their own number. They also stood in opposition to approximately 800 men who signed Lynn's largest antislavery petition, again a body of five times larger than their own.

If we compare only the shoemakers in each camp, antislavery men outnumber the anti-abolitionists. Of the approximately 900 cordwainers in Lynn in the 1830s, 301 signed antislavery petitions but only 46 subscribed to the attack on the women's equal rights memorial. The antislavery shoemakers comprised 53 percent of the petitioners; their opposites comprised 41 percent of the 171 anti-abolitionist protesters. Shoemakers therefore may be said to show a tendency to sympathize with blacks rather than to be hostile to them. Other craftsmen displayed the same tendency, and so did shoe manufacturers. In each instance anti-abolitionists claimed a smaller share of their whole protest constituency than antislavery men enjoyed in theirs (see Table 6–14). Only among fishermen, regarded as a semiskilled occupation, did anti-abolitionists dominate significantly (Table 6–14). Fishermen were 4.5 percent of the city's occupational structure, numbering between 58 (in 1832) and 93 (in 1841). Their numbers remain too small to bear the weight of a case for "mechanic" racism.

Why, then, did some Lynn citizens act so backwardly over the women's petition for black equality? The available data furnish no direct evidence to support any of the possible motivations suggested above, at least not any one of them alone. We could surmise that status anxiety, in terms of occupation and property ownership, was the cause of this reactionary behavior. We might just as well give some credence to the fears of racial amalgamation, for the statement in the anti-abolitionist petition makes this clear enough. And the sharp tone of reprimand to the female petitioners leaves little doubt that they had committed an unpardonable sin in the eyes of the anti-abolitionists. Again, status anxiety seems to be the answer. But this is a different breed of anxiety from that of displaced elites. It suggests a complex relationship to tradition. On the one hand, the tradition of equality derived from the political culture (namely the Declaration of Independence) seems to have been undervalued by the anti-abolitionists. On the other hand, the social traditions of male supremacy and white supremacy were retained; independence and self-reliance appeared to a minority of Lynn men to have been sullied, paradoxically, by a demand for black equal opportunity. Here is a case of ambivalence and uncertainty on the part of the anti-abolitionists in the face of proposed social change, weighted by their economic condition. Because their numbers were small, they gave indirect evidence that the abolitionists' faith in a constituency among the "bone and sinew" of society was well placed. Not even such perfectionists as the abolitionist leadership expected a score of 100 percent in winning adherents.

Other craftsmen and shoemakers in manufacturing towns added their real and symbolic sympathy for the black slave. The shoemaking towns of Haverhill and Leominster are only two of these communities. Last makers, shoe cutters, shoemakers, and shoe manufacturers comprised about 42 percent of a sample of 109 Haverhill petitioners opposing the annexation of Texas in 1837. In Leominster, one of Worcester County's industrial villages, cordwainers in a convivial celebration on March 30, 1839, included among their nineteen toasts one to "freedom of speech, freedom of the press, and freedom of the slave." Most of the toasts were of an anti-British and pro-Jackson tone, and they received loud bursts of applause from the lively crowd of shoemakers. The setting for this gala was symbolic of old master-and-journeyman relations. It was the "manufactory" of the local capitalist family illuminated for the occasion with 240 lights.[16] It seemed that even as the village was slipping over into the modern factory way of life, there was time and space left for mechanic and master, worker and boss, to celebrate republican ideals of liberty, fraternity, and equality. These festivities also symbolized the alliance in the antislavery constituency.

Another dimension of the social profile of the antislavery constituency is revealed by the petitioners' religious affiliation. Those of the signers for whom church membership could be determined were almost exclusively Protestant. Their preponderance reflects the social concerns and felt obligations

Table 6–16
Church Membership of 1830s Petitioners

Denomination	(N)	%
Baptist	90	19.0
Free Church of Worcester	1	.2
Congregationalist	75	15.8
Methodist	99	21.0
Presbyterian	96	20.3
Dutch Reformed	17	3.6
Protestant Episcopal	8	1.7
Unitarian	19	4.0
Quaker	43	9.1
Christian Union	17	3.6
Universalist	8	1.7
Total	473	100

stirred up by the Great Awakening. These concerns were bound together with the erosion of the producer ethic. Methodist, Presbyterian, Baptist, and Congregationalist church members hold the largest shares of the identified petitioners (see Table 6–16). If we use the compass of "ritualistic" and "pietistic" churches, the needle swings decisively to the latter. These were the churches that had pioneered in perfectionism, as William D. McLoughlin explains, and that were most prone to unite a drive for "inner perfection or holiness as personal union with God" with campaigns for perfection of the world "through the regeneration of everyone in it."[17] Among their objectives, abolition of slavery became paramount.

The sampled petitioners show catholicity within the world of Protestantism. Although pietistic churches dominate the statistics, there are also names of men in the nonevangelical or ritualistic Episcopal, Dutch Reformed, and Universalist churches. In part, the leader denominations here reflect the demography of the leading churches in particular cities. The republican ideology that informed the political and social conduct of farmers, artisans, and mechanics also shaped democratic church practices. The churches most affected by such influences were those with congregations of people in the working class and the new middle class.

Most attractive to working-class men and women were the Methodists and Baptists. Lynn's Methodist churches enjoyed a membership larger than the Congregationalist, Baptist, and Quaker denominations. This was especially true among shoemakers. Shoe manufacturing families such as the William and Isaac Bassetts flocked to the Society of Friends. It was no accident that their neighborhood in Lynn should be called Quaker Hill. Quaker strictures against slavery were long-standing and well known, and Friends' antislavery activity had made them a dependable contingent in the abolitionist movement.[18] But cordwainers, such as those who resided in the Woodend working-class area, made the Methodist church one of their distinctive institutions.[19]

Baptist and Methodist churches in the Northern states, and especially in New England, had become embroiled with their Southern brothers and sisters in controversy over slavery.[20] It was to be expected that men in those churches would be quick to sign antislavery petitions (see Table 6–16). We need only recall the effective antislavery leadership of such pastors as Asa Bronson in Fall River's Baptist Church, Phineas Crandall in Fall River and Orange Scott in Lowell and Springfield Methodist churches, and the roles of lay leaders such as James C. DeLong, the Wesleyan Methodist manufacturer and abolitionist in Utica, and members of the Mudge shoemaker family in Lynn's republican and Methodist Woodend. Thirty-three Methodists made up the largest group of known petitioning church members in Worcester, even though the leading denomination was the Congregationalist, with 665 members in its three churches. Presbyterian and Congregationalist petitioners followed the abolitionist leadership of their churches in Utica and Springfield. In the latter city, the Reverend Samuel Osgood, pastor of the First Church, made his home an Underground Railroad station for fugitive slaves, served as a vice president of the Hampden County Anti-Slavery Society, and used his church for the society's first meeting in 1838.[21] In Utica, the Reverend Oliver Wetmore, a Presbyterian minister steeped in the Puritan ethos passed down from his ancestor Jonathan Edwards, was a leader of the antislavery society and was one of the abolitionist victims of the 1835 "gentlemen's mob."[22]

Another way to discriminate among church members lies in the comparison of church affiliation and the class structure of the individual denominations. For aid in appreciating the complexities of the rank and file abolition profile, Table 6–17 fuses cultural and socioeconomic qualities of petitioners. This class-and-culture scale shows more skilled men in the Methodist, Baptist, and Universalist churches. Members of the middle class tend to gather in the Presbyterian, Congregationalist, Quaker, and Unitarian churches. The petitioners, while mainly in "pietistic" churches, also may be found on the other side of the fence, in ritualistic territory. Neither Puritan nor non-Puritan cultural heritage alone seems sufficient to explain the choices for abolitionism. Nevertheless, as Professor McLoughlin has shown, the perfectionist impulse must remain one of the weightiest components of motivation. That drive for inner and social improvement dovetails with motivational force to be inferred from Methodist and Baptist popularity and their ample antislavery activity: their members' republican and mechanic-class world views. Another side of the constituency is revealed by the congruence of middle-class men of means and churches which were generally cool toward abolitionism. However, the absence of many men from church membership lists prevents a firmer conclusion about the weight of evangelical religion upon the petitioners' antislavery choices.

The small numbers identified by church denomination in

Table 6–17
Occupational Structure of 1830s Petitioners by Their Churches

Occupational Group	Totals (N)	Totals %	Baptist (N)	Baptist %	Christian (N)	Christian %	Congregationalist (N)	Congregationalist %	Methodist (N)	Methodist %	Presbyterian (N)	Presbyterian %
Unskilled & Menial Svce.	14	3.2	6	7.2	2	11.8	2	2.9	2	2.2	1	1.1
Semiskilled & Service	5	1.1			1	5.7	1	1.5				
Propr-Mgr-Official	131	29.8	16	19.3	5	29.4	18	26.5	24	26.1	34	39.1
Skilled	198	45.1	47	56.6	7	41.2	22	32.4	56	60.9	33	37.9
Commerce & Sales	20	4.6	3	3.6	1	5.9	2	2.9	4	4.3	8	9.2
Semi-Professional	3	.7							2	2.2		
Professional	33	7.5	3	3.6			13	19.1	1	1.1	7	8.0
Farmers	29	6.6	8	9.6	1	5.9	9	13.2	3	3.3	3	3.4
Miscellaneous	6	1.4					1	1.5			1	1.1
Totals	439	100	83	19.0	17	3.9	68	15.5	92	20.9	87	19.8

Occupational Group	Totals		Dutch Reformed		Protestant Episcopal		Unitarian		Quaker		Univer-salist		Roman Catholic	
	(N)	%	(N)	%	(N)	%	(N)	%	(N)	%	(N)	%	(N)	%
Unskilled & Menial Svce.	14	3.2											1	100
Semiskilled & Service	5	1.1	1	6.7	1	12.5			1	2.3				
Propr-Mgr-Official	131	29.8	5	33.3	3	37.5	7	41.2	19	44.2				
Skilled	198	45.1	6	40.0	2	25.0	5	29.4	13	30.2	7	87.5		
Commerce & Sales	20	4.6					1	5.9	1	2.3				
Semi-Professional	3	.7			1	12.5								
Professional	33	7.5	3	20.0	1	12.5	3	17.6	2	4.7				
Farmers	29	6.6					1	5.9	4	9.3				
Miscellaneous	6	1.4							3	7.0	1	12.5		
Totals	439	100	15	3.4	8	1.8	17	3.9	43	9.8	8	1.8	1	.2

the petition sample may well reflect the low level of male church activity in the antebellum period. The petitioners excluded for lack of linkable data could have been among the unaffiliated men. In Utica, for example, women outnumbered men in each of four churches in the 1820s and 1830s. Seventy-two percent of the converts admitted to the Whitesboro Baptist Church during the Finney-led revivalism were women. But Mary P. Ryan points out that women comprised less than 51.3 percent of the combined populations of Utica and Whitesboro in 1838. Other historians, too, have demonstrated the widespread "feminization" of American antebellum churches.[23]

Some of the unidentified men probably were heirs to deism and secular radicalism, which had been popular among artisans and tradesmen in the late eighteenth and early nineteenth centuries. There may have been few nominal Paineites by the late 1830s, but the legacy of Paine's popularity and his philosophy probably was expressed in the spirit of the decade.

Secular radicalism among workingmen's groups seems to have been as potent a motivation for antislavery activity as evangelical religion was for other groups. In New York City there is ample evidence that radical republican artisans and shopkeepers participated in petition activity. However, these men appear to have been the adherents of George Henry Evans, who distrusted and opposed such abolitionist leaders and evangelical reformers as Arthur and Lewis Tappan, the wealthy financial angels of the antislavery movement and of the benevolence establishment in general. These leaders lost Paineite and Workingmen's support for abolition petitions between 1831 and 1834 because secular radicals suspected them of trying to unite church and state and of using moral reform to subvert republican ideals.

At the same time the upper-income, evangelical component of the antislavery constituency of the early 1830s had begun to slip away by the end of the decade. Arthur Tappan's appeal to pious followers for support of the antislavery movement was met with coolness and with the rebuke that "the abolitionist body was largely composed of irreligious men, some of infidel sentiments." Meanwhile, New York City artisans and shopkeepers, including the radicals, returned to the antislavery constituency and continued to be its base through the end of the decade. Their loyalty to the movement reinforced the assertion that the "bone and sinew" classes bore the abolitionist movement on their shoulders. Their reaffiliation probably compensated for any loss of the evangelically inspired abolitionists through the failure of the moral sausion tactic.

The shift within New York's antislavery constituency corresponds to the portrait presented in Table 6–17. The New York Workingmen and other artisans and shopkeepers, and the New England and upstate New York petitioners in the more plebeian churches, all shared both an outlook on economic and social conditions and a fealty to democratic republican ideals. This qualitative change in the ranks of abolitionism continued to exert pressure against the walls of political purism and one-ideaism that sealed the Liberty party of the 1840s in a household of dedicated and pious reformers.

Abolitionism, as we have seen in this chapter, drew its constituency from a broad sector of Americans. It was not the sectarian preserve of disgruntled and displaced New England elites. Sons and daughters of the old mercantile families, with deep roots in their communities, joined with the new energetic manufacturing class. But no longer can the antislavery movement be regarded as middleclass alone. The new factory workers were represented in the coalition alongside of the artisans and mechanics, and the farmers, as well as the middle classes of the cities. Those who were most vocal and adamant in opposition to the abolitionists and their racial egalitarianism, as in Lynn, proved to be a confused and insecure minority. They had interests inimical to those of the old "gentlemen of property and standing," yet aligned themselves with these upper-class scions fearful of "amalgamation." Moreover, these Lynn anti-abolitionists appeared to share the elite's fear of women's public and organized defiance of age-old authoritarianism. In the end, the profile of the antislavery constituency suggests that these backward elements were not decisive. The rank and file of abolitionism appeared to represent the hopes and desires of most Americans, of all ages, and especially across the divisions of economic condition and class. The profile points to a consensus capable of realizing abolition's goals.

NOTES

1. Paul Goodman, "A Guide to American Church Membership Data before the Civil War," *Historical Methods Newsletter* 10 (Fall 1977): 183–87; Goodman, "The Politics of Industrialism: Massachusetts, 1830–1870," in Richard L. Bushman, ed., *Uprooted Americans: Essays to Honor Oscar Handlin* (Boston: Little, Brown, 1979), p. 167; Mary P. Ryan, "A Women's Awakening: Evangelical Religion and the Families of Utica, New York, 1800–1840," *American Quarterly* 30 (Winter 1978): 602–23; Barbara Welter, "The Feminization of American Religion, 1800–1860," in Mary Hartman and Lois W. Banner, eds., *Clio's Consciousness Raised: New Perspectives in the History of Women* (New York: Harper and Row, 1974), pp. 137–57.

2. Robert W. Doherty, *Society and Power: Five New England Towns, 1800–1860* (Amherst: University of Massachusetts Press, 1977), p. 80.

3. See Michael B. Katz, "Social Class in North American Urban History," *Journal of Interdisciplinary History* 11 (Spring 1981): 579–605.

4. Peter Knights, *The Plain People of Boston, 1830–1860: A Study in City Growth* (New York: Oxford University Press, 1971), Appendix.

5. Utica City Directory, 1837–38.

6. See chapter 10, "Masters and Journeymen," in Howard B. Rock, *Artisans of the New Republic* (New York: New York University Press, 1979), pp. 265–69, for evidence of wage earner/master ratios of three to one and four to one in Jeffersonian times.

7. John Jentz, "The Antislavery Constituency in Jacksonian New York City," *Civil War History* 27 (June 1981): 106.

8. Thomas L. Dublin, "Women at Work: The Transformation of Work and Community in Lowell, Massachusetts, 1826–1860," (Ph.D. dissertation, Columbia University, 1975), p. 95.

9. Ibid., pp. 98–99, 105–106; Thomas Man, *Picture of a Factory Village* (Providence, 1833); 1845 estimate cited in Philip S. Foner, ed., *The Factory Girls* (Urbana: University of Illinois Press, 1977), p. 278.

10. Cf. Edward Pessen, *Riches, Class and Power before the Civil War* (Lexington, Mass.: D. C. Heath, 1973), pp. 36–39; Knights, *Plain People of Boston*, pp. 78–102.

11. John T. Cumbler, *Working-Class Community in Industrial America: Work, Leisure and Struggle in Two Industrial Cities, 1880–1930* (Westport, Conn.: Greenwood Press, 1979), p. 104.

12. Joseph G. Rayback, "The American Workingman and the Antislavery Crusade," *Journal of Economic History* 3 (November 1943), 152–163.

13. John R. Commons characterized the American labor movement as being narrowly concerned with "bread and butter" gains through the bargaining process in a marketplace relationship with employers. His critics have insisted that he underestimated class conflicts and denied working-class consciousness. They also charge that Commons failed to consider "the labor movement in its larger economic, political and social setting." Working class participation in the antislavery movement went beyond the boundaries fixed by Commons and his associates. See Commons and others, *History of American Labour in the United States*, vol. 1, (New York: Macmillan, 1918), p. 20; Alan Dawley, *Class and Community: The Industrial Revolution in Lynn* (Cambridge: Harvard University Press, 1976), pp. 180–84; Philip S. Foner, *History of the Labor Movement in the United States*, vol. 1, (New York: International Publishers, 1947), pp. 10–11.

14. Paul Faler, "Workingmen, Mechanics and Social Change: Lynn, Massachusetts, 1800–1860" (Ph.D. dissertation, University of Wisconsin, 1971), p. 476.

15. *The Liberator*, March 1, 1839.

16. Petition of Alfred Kittridge and 386 others, "Male Citizens: of Haverhill, Mass.," undated (ca. 1837), National Archives RG233, HR25A-H1.1 (Box 613), Bundle 12; Fitchburg (Mass.) *Sentinel,* April 3, 1839, courtesy of Donald M. Scott.

17. William G. McLoughlin, "Pietism and the American Character," *American Quarterly* 17 (Summer 1965): 167.

18. Faler, "Workingmen, Mechanics and Social Change," pp. 99–105, 201–13.

19. Thomas Drake, *Quakers and Slavery in America* (New Haven: Yale University Press, 1950), pp. 158–59.

20. Gilbert H. Barnes, *The Antislavery Impulse, 1830–1844* (New York: D. Appleton-Century, 1933), p. 91.

21. Mason A. Green, *Springfield, 1636–1886. History of Town and City* (Boston: 1888), p. 442.

22. Leonard L. Richards, "Gentlemen of Property and Standing: Anti-abolition Mobs in Jacksonian America (New York: Oxford University Press, 1970), p. 139.

23. Ryan, "A Women's Awakening," p. 603. See note 1 above.

CHAPTER 7

The 1830s Antislavery Constituency: Political Profile

Just as antislavery petitioners as a group reflected diverse ages, birthplaces, economic standings, and religions, so did they vary in their political thinking.

It must be stated at the outset that only a minority of all the male population in the cities subscribed to the abolitionist protests. In Utica, for example, an estimate of the data in the 1835 census shows about 3,600 men from fifteen to over sixty years of age. Only 273 names appeared on a September 26, 1837, petition for abolishing slavery in the District of Columbia (see Appendix B, Table B–3). In Massachusetts, too, petitioners represented small percentages of the males between fifteen and sixty. In the mid-1830s that age bracket was filled by about 1,800 in Worcester, 2,500 in Springfield, and 2,300 in Lynn. The largest 1837 and 1838 petitions in Springfield and Worcester enlisted 21 and 22 percent of those men. In Lynn, 860 legal voters (37 percent) outperformed the others by entering their names on one 1838 petition to rescind the congressional gag rule. Yet even this clear expression of democratic consciousness, it must be conceded, stands as the viewpoint of a statistical minority. Responses on the substantive antislavery issues were even less emphatic.

Although women played an even more impressive role in

the petition campaign in these same cities, they did not do much better in terms of their portion of the population. The largest of their remonstrances analyzed in this study garnered 1,409 signatures in Lowell, on June 6, 1836. It called for the abolition of slavery in the District of Columbia, and represents a total of 20 percent of Lowell's women between fifteen and sixty years of age. Lynn female petitioners reached 38 percent of that city's mature women with 912 signatures on the District abolition petition (see Appendix B, Table B–2).[1] One might speculate that antislavery sentiment flourished more among Lynn's numerous homebound female shoe binders than among their working-class sisters in Lowell's mills. But clearly there is a hint there of possible heightened working-class republicanism.

A more telling comparison of petitioners to population is in the ratio of petitioners to voters. Men frequently labeled themselves as "legal voters" or "citizens" in writing up the message in the petition. While thus separating themselves from women and from foreign-born men, they also appear to be giving emphasis to their potential electoral roles. The effectiveness of the petitions had already been acknowledged by the anger of Southern Congressmen. Further respect for these paper protests, although in negative form, was reflected in the gag rule. But few contemporaries perceived or emphasized the political power waiting to be released from the body of signers, except for the incipient political abolitionists such as Birney, Leavitt, Whittier, Stanton, and Alvan Stewart. This potential may be appreciated by observing the ratios of the most popular petitions to the number of voters in the sampled cities (see Appendix B, Table B–3). From 45 to 76 percent of the electorate in Lynn and in Worcester appear to be an abolitionist constituency, crossing party lines. The same comparison in the New York towns reveals that abolitionists there trailed behind their Bay State counterparts. The largest petitions in the sampled cities represented only 8 to 20 percent of the voters.[2]

We would be better acquainted with the beliefs of the antislavery constituency if we could join some of the men at their polling places. But missing poll books and poll lists hamper our purpose. Such records do not exist for any of the cities chosen for this study. However, lists of voters have been found for two towns of Worcester County where citizens signed antislavery petitions. We may therefore reverse the linking process and begin with the voter list, then identify some of the names in it with antislavery petitioners. The voter lists for Harvard and Northborough were compiled in response to a questionnaire sent out by the county Whig leadership in an effort to calculate the party's prospects in the upcoming 1840 elections. The two towns were close enough to the city of Worcester to suggest the political climate in and around the metropolis.

Harvard and Northborough were part of the county's farming areas, but each contained some relatively small-scale manufacturing firms. Sheep raising was a significant activity in the county, making wool a marketable product in both towns. Harvard, with the larger population of the two—1556 to Northborough's 1224—trailed in the value of manufactured goods. Northborough's two small cotton mills employed 17 males and 31 females who turned out 200,000 yards of cotton goods valued at $30,400. In the same town, boots and shoes valued at $30,720 were produced by 50 males and 25 females. Harvard's footwear production, by 16 male and 8 female workers, was worth $11,000. Its three paper mills, employing 9 males and 2 females, turned out a product valued at $12,750. Other manufacturing brought Harvard's workforce in that sector to 48 persons, Northborough's to 135.[3]

Politically they were Whig towns. Election results showed that Northborough's Whigs held a sizable lead until the Free Soil party overwhelmed both them and the Democrats. Harvard voters, on the other hand, began to move away from the Whigs in 1835. By 1839, Marcus Morton, the Democratic candidate for governor, polled 160 votes there to Edward Everett's 122. Democrats held this lead down to 1848 when Free Soilers gained a plurality.[4]

In 1840, the poll lists compiled by the Whigs showed 321 voters in Harvard and 245 in Northborough. These were divided as follows: 182 Whigs, 38 "Loco[foco]s," and 25 "Doubtful" in Northborough; 142 "R[eform]" or Whigs, 124, "T[ories]" or Democrats, and 29 "X" or doubtful in Harvard. The names of 26 Shaker "voters" who did not cast ballots were excluded from Harvard's list. It is interesting to note that 20 of Northborough's Whig voters appeared to defect in the 1839 elections, and 30 in the spring 1840 election when a selectman was elected by the Democrats. Similar departures from Harvard's Whig ranks occurred in other 1839 and 1840 elections. Whigs in both towns blamed "temperance legislation" (the 1838 restrictive fifteen-gallon law) for their losses. Harvard's local Whigs added that voters' objections to "the militia" and "railroads" shifted votes to Morton for governor in 1839.[5] These two are not the sort of issues that ethnocultural determinists could cite in support of their theories of voter behavior. Although temperance was such an issue, Whig defections over it, especially among ethnically homogeneous voters, tend to undermine such determinism. The voters' objections on the ostensibly economic issues appear to be grounded in principles of personal liberty and equal opportunity. Opposition to privilege and monopoly seems to be involved in the militia and railroad questions, and suggests that class attitudes played a role in these statewide contests.

Slavery and the right of petition were two issues upon which citizens of the two towns voted their moral concerns. In 1838 and 1839 voters and their wives did so by adding their names to anti-gag petitions. These protests were themselves buried by the gag rule. But they reveal notable numbers of local Democrats who, by signing, broke ranks with the national party. For our purposes they furnish names which may be linked to a crude social profile. Harvard provided 63 male signatures and Northborough 121. Of their known party designations, 28 were Democrats (20.7 percent), and 107 were Whigs (79.3 percent). The heavy Whig presence comes as no surprise, for the party cherished an image of itself as the "conscience" party, the guardian of society's moral and economic virtues. But neither should a Democratic showing of 20 percent come as a surprise. Despite the acquiescence of that party's Northern leadership to slavery and the violations of abolitionists' civil liberties by Democratic officeholders, the party claimed to stand for personal liberty and unfettered opportunity in the unfolding capitalism of the 1830s and 1840s. As tension over slavery disturbed the Democrats, interference with a First Amendment right like petitioning obviously offended significant numbers of rank and filers. In the main, Harvard and Northborough voters' names on anti-gag petitions furnish direct evidence, heretofore missing, to affirm the Whig political complexion of the antislavery constituency in the late 1830s.

With the Whig party laying claim to a moral stewardship, and popular in small towns, it is no wonder that abolitionists counted on its adherents to support their cause. The social composition of the voter-petition sampling of Harvard and Northborough tends to confirm the abolitionist description of their constituency as the yeoman farmers and mechanics of the New England towns. In the two towns under consideration, occupations were found for fifty-nine men. Thirty-one were farmers and sixteen were artisans. Among the Whig signers farmers were two-thirds of the known occupations. From that sample we learn that among the small number of known Democrats were four farmers, four artisans, and two middle-class men. Such data could very well have persuaded eager Liberty party activists that their constituency for the 1840s resided in the yeomen and the mechanics of such places as Harvard and Northborough.[6]

As if it had become an extension of the Whig party, the Liberty party was regarded as the "merely sectarian, moralistic and evangelistic" one—a household of dedicated and pious moral reformers.[7] But that view fails to consider the tendencies and movements within the party that were taking it toward Free Soilism and Democratic social and economic planks. In 1846, for example, the Liberty party in New York's western counties endorsed Free Soil principles exemplified by George Henry Evans's National Reform Association. The eventual dissolution of the Liberty party and its renascence in the Free Soil party would not diminish a conscientious commitment to abolition. In fact the Liberty party cadres remained the conscience of the new antislavery coalition. They had adopted a tactic that coincided with the pressures brought upon the Whig and Democratic parties for greater antislavery action. The resultant Free Soil party represented an alliance of evangelistically inspired perfectionists with pragmatic land reformers, all pursuing democratic republican ends. The social base of the coalition appeared to be an enlargement of the 1830s antislavery rank and file. If not the "Bible politics" of 1840, the coalition was an advance over what abolitionists had then scorned as tawdry politicking.

By 1844 the original Whig base of the abolitionist party had departed, leaving a vacuum that ex-Democrats had begun to fill. In the Whig Worcester *Massachusetts Spy*, John Milton Earle charged that an alliance of Liberty and Democratic parties was forming against the Whigs. By 1848, however, Earle severed his ties with the Whig party, joined the Free Soil movement, and made the *Spy* an organ of Free Soilism.[8] The Haverhill abolitionist and former Whig legislator John Greenleaf Whittier looked to the Democrats rather than the Whigs for "more hope"in the 1848 election. "They are bolder, freer, and less influenced by conservatism," he wrote.[9] Whittier must have been encouraged by the split in Democratic ranks over slavery extension engendered by the Texas annexation issue. It deepened after the Mexican War and the failure of the Wilmot Proviso. In New York, traditionally Democratic counties became Free Soil strongholds in the 1848 contests. A coalition of antislavery Democrats, Whigs, and Liberty men was being formed. In New Hampshire, the Democratic-Liberty affinities were made evident during the late 1840s even though some Whigs in the Liberty party were returning to their old political allegiance in that same period.[10]

In New York's 1846 gubernatorial election, the Liberty party approved Free Soil and the ten-hour working day on public works. A year later the party's candidate for lieutenant governor won the support of the anti-rent (anti-monopoly) forces.[11] When Owen Lovejoy went east from Illinois to campaign for Liberty candidates in Massachusetts' Fourth Congressional District in 1846, he shrewdly assessed the changing party relationships: "The Whigs and Democrats put up men who are well-known for their anti-slavery sentiment. . . . The Whigs sail just as close to the Liberty bark as they can, to suck the wind out of our sails. . . . But the Liberty party here has shown that it cannot be induced to go and worship the idols that the Whigs have set up."[12]

The New York State Liberty party meeting in Utica in 1848 made vivid the movement toward alliance with antislavery Democrats. Following adjournment of the abolition gathering, its delegates marched to a convention of New York antislavery Democrats, also in Utica, and "announced that the abolitionists were at their door knocking for admission."[13]

But even earlier, the potential antislavery vote of Democrats was suggested by Lynn office-seekers in the November 1836 election. Four slates of candidates for state representatives entered the race: Democrats, Jackson Democrats, Whigs, and Independent Mechanics. The polls of the ten Whigs ranged from 412 to 545, and they were elected. Twelve Democrats polled from 342 to 347; a dozen Jacksonians attracted a consistent vote of 321, and Independent Mechanics, 39 to 43.

The names of men in each of the four parties showed up on antislavery petitions between 1836 and 1839, including one against annexation of Texas, another against the gag rule, and two against slavery and the slave trade in the District of Columbia. Perhaps surprisingly, the best showing was made by the Jacksonians: nine of their twelve names appeared on the abolitionists' petitions. They were followed by eight of the twelve Democrats (two of whom had been Anti-Masonic candidates in 1832); six of ten Whigs, and six of twelve Mechanics. Only one of the candidates, a Mechanic, appeared on the anti-abolitionist letter published in the *Liberator*. Lynn's voters appear to have preferred Democrats over Whigs and to have approved of men who had also backed the abolitionists. In this particular contest, Whigs won, and overshadowed the larger Democratic and urban working-class constituency that was destined to become much more united and visible by the late 1840s.[14] It is notable that in 1832, five of eight Whigs were to become antislavery petitioners. Five of eight Anti-Masons and only three of eight Jacksonians were to sign 1836–37 petitions. The Anti-Masonic victory in the election suggested a strong antimonopoly and antiaristocratic voter preference.

Yet another indicator of the strength of antislavery sentiment among 1830s Democrats comes from Whittier. He, like many other abolitionists, was enthusiastic over the Massachusetts Legislature's March 1837 resolution against the congressional gag rule and was in favor of using congressional power to abolish slavery and the slave trade in the District of Columbia. Whittier wrote to a friend, "The legislature is abolitionized, the whole state is coming." As for the Democrats, Whittier wrote, "The Van Buren men are persuaded to look to the people of Massachusetts, and not to orders from Washington. And they have done as we advised: to save themselves they have joined hands with the abolitionists."[15] Although Whittier's exuberance was perhaps naive and premature, the important point in his statement is that Democratic legislators heeded not only the abolitionists but their own constituents. These Democrats were not alone in moving toward party realignment. Ronald Formisano has revealed a similar phenomenon among Whigs in Massachusetts, although this evidence is derived from opposition rather than from support. He writes that party managers attempted to prevent the Whigs from taking open positions against slavery and in favor of the ten-hour law. Their actions suggest that there were movements among the party rank and file in support of those positions as early as 1833.[16]

The sprigs of new political formations were overshadowed, to some extent, by the 1847 Macedon Lock (New York) convention of the Liberty League. This was a creation of William Goodell and other abolitionists who acknowledged the severe limitations of the Liberty party's "one-ideaism." Their goal was to form a new Liberty party that would embrace a greater number of reforms. Goodell had unsuccessfully attempted such a transformation in 1845. Now he linked the abolition of slavery to a full-blown program of "destruction of the minor monopolies and aristocracies subsidized by and sustaining it." As Goodell explained years later, the widened platform would include issues such as free trade, free public lands, limitation of land ownership, inalienable homesteads, "abolition of all legalized monopolies and castes," workingmen's rights, and retrenchment of government expenses. These had been some of the principal measures advocated by the Locofocos and other radical Democrats. Any antislavery society could limit itself to abolition of "one form of oppression and robbery," Goodell went on. But "civil government" could not be so circumscribed. "Protection of *all* the rights of *all* men," Goodell wrote, was a divine ordinance that civil governments must follow. Such a government must seek "universal equality and impartial justice to all." This included, but was not limited to, the abolition of slavery. Goodell reminded the Macedon Lock convention that its members would be remiss if they put in abeyance their convictions of the moral wrongfulness "of corn laws, cloth laws, and other legislative devices for grinding the face of the poor," in order to vote only for "the opposers of chattel enslavement." Goodell pointed out that the British government that abolished West Indies chattel slavery was, at the same time, "starving the people of Ireland, . . . crushing the operatives of Birmingham and perpetrating other moral outrages," some of which were against the emancipated blacks themselves. Goodell touched on exposed nerve when he asserted that the British importation of East Indian laborers into the West Indies cut the wages of black workers there and brought "helpless destitution upon both negroes and coolies, thus reviving, though without chattelhood, the closest possible resemblance to the slave trade!"

The eradication of iniquity and oppression required a turnout of a broad electorate at the ballot box. Arguing for a multireform Liberty party, Goodell edged close to the radical Democrat and former Workingmen's programs. More immediately pressing was the need to convince abolitionists to recognize the potentially large constituency of "the masses of men who feel that they have wrongs of their own to redress."[17]

Goodell's prescriptions reflected what in fact was happening in Massachusetts, New Hampshire, New York, and other states. Texas annexation and a sterner proslavery line in the Democratic party were splitting the party's membership. Conscience Whigs became increasingly uncomfortable with their party's failure to oppose slavery. Antislavery Democrats, fusing the party's reform program with a desire to curb the spread of slavery, were growing stronger and seemed to be approaching Goodell's ideal of a reform party. In 1844 and 1845, Massachusetts Democrats stayed away from the polls or helped to swell Liberty votes. In 1846 and 1847, Liberty candidates in Massachusetts won the endorsement of workingmen's groups. Reinhard Johnson concluded that from 1840 to about 1845–46, the Massachusetts Liberty party rested on a social and religious base like that of the Whigs, but from about 1845 to 1848 the antislavery party drew its support from a social base like that of the Democratic party.[18]

By appealing to Democrats to vote for Liberty candidates in Massachusetts, abolitionists appeared to be recognizing the latent power of an urban industrial working class and farmer constituency. Goodell and Whittier were not alone in extending an indirect invitation to that social base through their arguments for a reform party and/or an informal alliance with Democrats. Joshua Leavitt, editor of *The Emancipator* and petition campaign manager in the 1830s, added his influential voice. Leavitt's editorials made a direct appeal to Democrats to switch to the Liberty party.

Another direct appeal to workingmen is contained in an open letter from an abolitionist writing from Amesbury "To the workingmen of Essex [County]." "As one of your number," the writer argued that the degradation of useful labor by slaveowners diminished the worth of the Northern workingmen. "Slavery has crushed the working population of the South—white and black—and it is waging a warfare with Northern freedom. . . . Our first great business, as was that of the men of '76, is to secure LIBERTY," he wrote. The strong tones of republicanism in his appeal are spread across two columns of the newspaper. Finally, the writer invoked one of the most profound and precious concepts of nineteenth century American working-class consciousness. He signed himself "Yours, for the dignity of labor."[19] Such an appeal could not but be accorded a hearing in changing cities like Boston or Worcester as well as in a myriad of factory towns altering Northeastern landscapes and labor relations, and could also help to salvage the reputations of abolitionists who, too often, were identified by some working-class leaders as callous to the wrongs manufacturers heaped upon artisans and laborers.

Abolitionists in the 1840s, seeking Democrats' and workingmen's votes, appeared less ambivalent than they had in the 1830s. Ten years earlier Goodell and others had recognized the importance of workingmen to the antislavery crusade. However, the Utica editor appeared to equivocate on workers' rights. At that time mechanic and artisan interests appeared to coincide with those of manufacturers and some merchants as opposed to "aristocrats" of the North and the South. Whittier's Essex County newspaper cogently defined that elite as "the Lords Spiritual of Andover, and the Lords Temporal of Boston." In the 1840s a marked change was reflected in the epithetical "Lords of the Lash and Lords of the Loom" who ruled over Southern cotton fields and Northern cotton factories.[20]

Uniquely perspicacious concerning relations between the working class and abolitionism was Nathaniel P. Rogers, the editor of the Concord, New Hampshire, *Herald of Freedom*. As early as 1843 he had proposed a more serious commitment of abolitionists to Northern working men. Rogers, too, invoked the dignity of labor in advocating that working men abolish slavery. But, he insisted, they must first emancipate themselves from their bondage to capital. Abolitionists could aid greatly if they were to demand "liberty for New Hampshire day-laborers" as well as for Southern slaves. Rogers's forceful analysis of the relations of Yankee industrial capitalism trod heavily on the tender toes of middle-class abolitionists, who regarded him as an anathema. Like the acutely sensitive writer Herman Melville, he depicted machinery—"labor saving machinery"—not as the engine of plenty and progress trumpeted by middle-class spokesmen, but as the enslaver, fettering the worker. "Monopoly and capital seize on the labor saving machine, and wield it to the poor man's destruction," Rogers charged.[21] Melville described a New England paper mill in ways that set him apart from most of his fellow artists and members of his class and kin: "Machinery—that vaunted slave of humanity—here stood menially served by humans, who served mutely and cringingly as the slave serves the Sultan. The girls do not so much seem accessory wheels to the general machinery as mere cogs to the wheels."[22]

In 1836, the *Essex Gazette* had already caught the drift of early industrial capitalist production relations. Perhaps the Lowell mill women's strike that summer illuminated the new relationship. At any rate the journal, in a county heavily invested with shoe manufacturing, defended and approved of "the real worth of the mechanic[s]" who resisted the burdens placed upon them by the "aristocracy." The Haverhill newspaper made explicit the connection between workers and abolition of slavery in an editorial entitled "Aristocracy vs. Abolition." The editor perceived a confrontation of the "Aristocracy of the North" against "the middle interest men." These were defined as the "mechanics, farmers and labor classes" that filled "our ranks of abolition." The editor asserted that the main question facing the nation was "the right of the laborer, whether white or black, to the fruits of his hard toil."[23]

Working-class spokesmen had sharply made clear their priorities. William West had expressed a balanced formula in 1846, "Down with all slavery—chattel and wages." The Boston *Weekly Reformer*, on the other hand, gave priority to the cause of the "white slave—the mechanic—operative—day laborer, that suffers much from the *same cause* that galls the southern slave." But Goodell, in 1837, like Garrison, Wendell Phillips, and Judge John Jay, reversed the priorities. He called upon free Northern laborers to postpone redressing their grievances. "When the heavier oppressions of slavery are removed, the way will be prepared to remove more effectively the lighter burdens that press on the free," Goodell wrote in reply to the Boston *Reformer*. The fight against slavery, he maintained, set a precedent and established principles useful to "all oppressed laborers without distinction of color." And that was why, he continued, "the northern aristocracy have bent their bows to shoot at the advocates of the poor slaves."[24] Not all abolitionists were like Judge Jay, Goodell seemed to plead. Nonetheless, the message to workingmen was: wait!

That dilatory policy changed markedly in the 1840s as the abolitionist constituency was enlarged by national events. The display of aggression by the "slave power" in the annexation of Texas, and in the war against Mexico, split the two major parties. Antislavery Democrats and Conscience Whigs found common ground with Liberty men moving toward broader platforms. The Free Soil party that erupted in 1848 demonstrated the widening circles of antislavery concern and workingmen's discontent, along with the failure of Whig and Democratic leadership to maintain the hegemony desired by both Southern planters and the Northern commercial and manufacturing elites. Although the emerging alliance was flawed by morally imperfect motivations and by white supremacist interests, the Free Soil platform offered a program of republican moral and socioeconomic progress: "Free Soil, Free Labor, Free Men, Free Speech." The 290,000 votes cast for Martin Van Buren and Charles Francis Adams made it impossible ever again to ignore slavery or its extension in party politics. Nor would the demands of industrial workers be shunted off for long after 1848. A major qualitative change had been achieved thanks to the abolitionist agitation of the 1830s, the Liberty party, and labor's challenge in the 1840s. But so too did the slave system's aggressive elites and their Northern allies' accommodationist strategy hasten the political transformations.

NOTES

1. United States Census, Massachusetts, 1830 and 1840.

2. A majority of Utica's twelve hundred voters were reported by Henry B. Stanton to have signed a petition to Congress after Weld spoke there in March 1836. That petition may be the one that I located at the National Archives; dated March 21, 1836, it contains three hundred signatures. Additional pages, with some names, may have been lost. See report in *Proceedings of the 1st Annual Meeting, New York State Anti-Slavery Society* (Utica, 1836), and John L. Myers, "The Beginning of Anti-Slavery Agencies in New York State, 1833–1836," *New York History* 43 (April 1962), p. 171.

3. "Voters in Northboro, Nov. 1840" And "A List of Voters in the Town of Harvard" (ca. 1840), Worcester County Papers, Massachusetts Collection, American Antiquarian Society; *The Massachusetts Spy*, April 1838.

4. *The Massachusetts Spy*, November 11, 1835, November 1840; *The Emancipator and Free American*, December 1, 1842, November 23, 1843, January 5, 1849.

5. Whig Committees, Town of Harvard and Town of Northborough, reply to Nathan Heard, Whig County Committee, on questionnaires of May 1, 1840, in Worcester County Collection, American Antiquarian Society.

6. United States Census, Massachusetts, 1850.

7. Daniel Walker Howe, *The Political Culture of the American Whigs* (Chicago: University of Chicago Press, 1979), p. 18.

8. *The Massachusetts Spy*, June 21, June 28, July 19, 1848; James Eugene Mooney, "Antislavery in Worcester County: A Case Study," (Ph.D. dissertation, Clark University, 1971), pp. 152–53.

9. Reinhard O. Johnson, "The Liberty Party in Massachusetts, 1840–1848: Antislavery Third Party Politics in The Bay State," *Civil War History* 28 (September 1982): 255.

10. Richard H. Sewell, *Ballots for Freedom: Antislavery Politics in the United States, 1837–1860* (New York: Oxford University Press, 1976), pp. 127–30; Reinhard O. Johnson, "The Liberty Party in New Hampshire, 1840–1848: Antislavery Politics in the Granite State," *Historical New Hampshire* 33 (Summer 1978): 123–58.

11. Alan Kraut, "The Liberty Men of New York: Political Abolitionism in New York State, 1840–1848," (Ph.D. dissertation, Cornell University, 1975), p. 135.

12. Edward Magdol, *Owen Lovejoy, Abolitionist in Congress* (New Brunswick: Rutgers University Press, 1967), p. 79.

13. Kraut, "The New York Liberty Party," p. 147.

14. Lynn *Record*, November 16, 1836.

15. John B. Pickard, ed., *The Letters of John Greenleaf Whittier*, vol. 1 (Cambridge: Harvard University Press, 1975), p. 229.

16. Ronald P. Formisano, *The Transformation of Political Culture: Massachusetts Parties, 1790s–1840s* (New York: Oxford University Press, 1983), p. 329.

17. Goodell's *Address of the Macedon Convention . . .* (Albany, 1847) in Jane H. Pease and William H. Pease, eds., *The Antislavery Argument* (Indianapolis: Bobbs-Merrill, 1965), pp. 427–39; and his 1845 views at Port Byron, New York, in Aileen S. Kraditor, *Means and Ends in American Abolitionism: Garrison and His Critics on Strategy and Tactics: 1834–1850* (New York: Pantheon, 1969), pp. 153–54.

18. R. O. Johnson, The Liberty Party in Massachusetts," p. 255.

19. A. L. Bayley, "To the Workingmen of Essex," Amesbury, October 6, 1846, in *The Emancipator*, October 21, 1846.

20. *The Liberator*, February 4, 1837; *The Friend of Man*, August 25, September 8, 1836.

21. Rogers, cited in Eric Foner, *Politics and Ideology in the Age of the Civil War* (New York: Oxford University Press, 1980), p. 68.

22. "The Tartarus of Maids," *Selected Writings of Herman Melville* (New York: Modern Library, 1952), p. 202.

23. Reprinted in *The Friend of Man*, August 25, September 8, 1836.

24. *The Liberator*, February 4, 1837.

CHAPTER 8

The Anti–Nebraska Act
Rank and File

The widening antislavery public of the late 1840s revealed some notable internal changes. By 1854 these would become marked features of a mass movement that would overturn the political parties. If the Liberty (antislavery) voters in the pre–Mexican War years showed a tendency to appear in New England manufacturing towns, the Free Soilers in 1848 made those signs of voter change indelible. That year the Free Soil party carried industrial Massachusetts cities such as Worcester, Fitchburg, Leominster, and Leicester; it garnered 40 percent of the votes in boot and shoemaking towns. Great numbers of Lynn artisans supported the party. In Boston it gained votes in native-born and in Irish immigrant precincts. In Utica, Van Buren and Adams ran ahead of the Democrats but behind the Whigs. The working-class and largely Irish Fourth Ward gave 35 percent of its votes to Free Soilers, a larger portion than in any of the other three wards. At a Worcester mass meeting on June 21, 1848, one reporter heard abolitionist and Whig Judge Charles Allen describe his withdrawal from the party as a protest to its nomination of Taylor. Then the great crowd heard his call for formation of a new party. The reporter noted that "press and ministry paid little attention" but that "the men from the shops who were the real rulers of the city" gave their full attention to the speech. Later that year Allen was elected to the first of two terms as a Free Soil congressman. Of fifty Free Soil representatives elected to the Massachusetts legislature, twenty were from Worcester County. Before the rally at Worcester's city hall adjourned, the men "adopted with shouts" a resolution proclaiming that "Massachusetts goes now and will forever go for free soil and free men, for free lips and a free press, for a free land and a free world." After Allen's speech the county witnessed a wave of organization of Free Soil and "freedom clubs." In the city of Worcester, eight hundred joined at a meeting chaired by John Milton Earle. Additional clubs were formed in Holden, Leicester, Millbury, Northbridge, and North Brookfield between June and November.[1]

The enthusiasm for Free Soil was a continuing response to antiplutocratic notions informing the party's earlier 1830s appeals. Class frictions rather than ethnocultural concerns were shaping political behavior. Lynn artisans, during the 1840s, based their opposition to slavery and their identification with the slave on their abhorrence of aristocracy and monopoly of the land. Lynn manufacturers were grouped with slaveowners as "lordly tyrants." Charles Sumner reinforced such concepts when he told the 1848 Free Soil convention that "the efforts to place the national government on the side of freedom have received little sympathy from corporations, or from persons largely interested in them." He asserted that "the money power has joined hands with the slavery power," reiterating a notion widespread among farmers and working men.[2]

These renewed outbursts of antislavery sentiment posed both problems and opportunities for abolitionist leaders. Many of them felt the need to adopt a plan of coalition in order to attract a mass following to a platform of non-extension. While many old-time radical abolitionists deplored this necessity to horse-trade with former opponents like Van Buren, most appeared resigned to the strategy. Many probably agreed with the central idea expressed by Owen Lovejoy. "The principle of Liberty is in this movement, undergird and surround it," he wrote. "The immediate object aimed at is one which we cordially approve, and the ultimate object is identical—the extinction of slavery."[3] Coalition became only one arrow in the abolitionist quiver, with all of them bowed against the whole body of slavery.

The tactic proved to be of variable utility. In 1848 Free Soil congressmen, state legislators, and two United States senators changed the complexion and purposes of government and parties. Whigs and Democrats, too, proclaimed their commitments to Free Soil ideals and, in 1849 and 1850, they succeeded in weaning many away from the new alliance. The compromise of that midcentury year was hailed as the final solution of the slavery question.

But the "peace" and "finality" were shattered irrevocably in January 1854 when Stephen A. Douglas of Illinois introduced the Nebraska Act in the Senate. An action that Douglas may have believed to be evenhanded statesmanship, the proposed law would repeal the sacred Missouri Compromise of 1820 and permit slavery to be established by "popular sovereignty" north of a line at 36° 30′. Among the results of this breathtaking assault on the root idea of Free Soil was the remobilization of the 1848 coalition. The illusory peace of 1850–54 was stripped down to reveal the unabated conflict between systems of slave labor and free labor.

The outcry in Northern communities against Douglas' bill seemed to come too little and too late. The bill became law in May. When popular protest did appear, however, it came as a powerful demonstration of mass indignation. Rallies of tens of thousands gathered to denounce the act as a violation of the nation's trust. During February and March 1854, from Maine to Wisconsin, mass meetings roared their slogans of support for Free Soil doctrine. Thousands assembled in Boston, New York, Philadelphia, Pittsburgh, Milwaukee, and Chicago, and in dozens of smaller cities such as Utica and Worcester.

The protest was as broad socially as it was geographically, crossing lines of class, creed, party, and ethnicity. Three thousand New England clergymen sent a petition to Congress. Outraged statements of Boston's commercial elite showed that despite their accommodations with Southern planters they understood where the irredeemable liabilities lay in their political ledgers. On March 14, New York City merchants, ministers, and lawyers filled the great Broadway Tabernacle in protest. Middle-class Germans, exiles because of their roles in the democratic 1848 revolution, were the first to rally. They assembled in Chicago to protest their senator's bill. German Marxists led by Joseph Weydemeyer joined the campaign and urged labor to take an active role. A March 1 meeting in New York City's Kleindeutschland adopted a resolution promoted by Weydemeyer, Gottlieb Kellner, and other Forty-eighters. It stressed the threat of an expansive slavery to free soil and free labor and pledged to continue protesting "both white and black slavery." Later that spring, meetings and parades of immigrant artisans, professionals, and merchants in New York demonstrated how deeply their republicanism was offended by the repeal of the Missouri Compromise.[4]

In one of labor's earliest protests five thousand native- and foreign-born "mechanics and workingmen" had gathered at the Broadway Tabernacle. They met to protest "the violation of the Missouri Compromise" and to state their "determined hostility to any further encroachments by the Slave Power on the rights of free labor in the territories secured by that compact." The call had been signed by builders, artisans in the building crafts, some merchants, architects, hat manufacturers, druggists, surveyors, blacksmiths, teamsters, brass founders, coppersmiths, printers, painters, cartmen, accountants, and "workmen engaged in various other businesses." A hint of multiethnic unity came in a statement sent to the House of Representatives by an otherwise unidentified "Society of Universal Democratic Republicanism." It claimed to be made up of native-born Americans, and "adopted citizens and political refugees." The society's resolution viewed every extension of slavery as "perilous to Republican Liberty."[5]

The concern that slavery's extension endangered citizenship, opportunity, and labor's rights was expressed by an Albany, New York, petition to Congress. This was a remonstrance from seventy-two "Workingmen of Eagle Foundry." Among the signers are names suggesting a variety of national origins: Irish, such as Patrick Toohey and Thomas Quin; Dutch, such as Erastus Van Benthuysen and Jas. Groesbeck; and Anglo-American, such as Matthew Bell, Johnson Kimball, and Ed Stevens.[6]

Groups of citizens prevailed upon local governments to voice their opposition to the Kansas-Nebraska bill. The Haverhill, Massachusetts, town meeting protested the measure in March 1854. Among its objections was one to the bill's "gross departure from the policy of the founders of the Republic, which was to limit and restrain with a view to its final extinction, and not to foster and extend Slavery." A Mendon, Massachusetts, town meeting unanimously denounced the bill. In the small town of De Witt only one refused to sign a petition, and in the other Worcester County towns voters were involved in a variety of actions, from signing petitions to mass meetings. One such assemblage was "a united congregation of the Evangelical churches" in Fitchburg. In Rome, New York, a mass meeting scheduled in February 1854 was considerably hampered by severely cold weather, but the call had been in the form of a petition signed by about four thousand Oneida County men. Similarly, in Worcester 1,193 men were reported to have signed an anti–Kansas-Nebraska remonstrance. They included John Davis, a noted Whig, Charles Allen, the Free Soil standard bearer and congressman, and John S. C. Knowlton, prominent Democrat and editor of that party's newspaper, the Worcester *Palladium*. In addition, the Worcester anti–Kansas-Nebraska mass meeting at the City Hall was chaired by Mayor Peter C. Bacon. Among the rally's vice presidents were Allen, Rev. Thomas Wentworth Higginson of the radical Free Church, the industrialist Ichabod Washburn, and Eli Thayer, later to become organizer of aggressive emigration to troubled Kansas.[7] Representative Allen addressed the City Hall audience. He reviewed past aggressions of the slave power and called on "laborers, Mechanics and Farmers" to unite in saving the country from further encroachments on its "cherished institutions which were won by the valor of our fathers."[8]

Examples of church involvement included a community meeting called by 1,500 citizens of Providence, Rhode Island. The gathering in the Beneficent Congregational Church protested the Kansas-Nebraska bill's opening of possible "renewed injuries" to the Indian tribes in the territories. Resolutions were offered in the name of liberty, humanity, and "the plighted public faith." Not far away, in Western, Rhode Island, a few weeks later, 840 Free Will Baptists in their quarterly meeting signed a petition protesting the Douglas bill as "a great moral wrong."[9]

Petitions reminiscent of the 1830s, bearing thousands of names, again rained on Congress in 1854. A sampling of this public action is contained in petitions from Utica, Rome, Schenectady, New Hartford, and Ogdensburgh (Oswegatchie), New York, and Fall River, Lynn, Springfield, and Worcester, Massachusetts. New Hartford and Ogdensburgh will be examined in more detail.

New Hartford Township, on Utica's southern boundary, included an early cotton manufacturing concern but was mainly a farming community. In its occupational structure farmers comprised 33 percent, and laborers (probably members of farm families) 27.5 percent. Factory employees made up 10.5 percent. Eight hundred and forty foreign-born people, almost all from Great Britian, were among the five thousand inhabitants. A bit more than half of the American-born were from New England states. The Presbyterian and Protestant Episcopal were the largest churches, followed closely by the Methodist Episcopal. Small congregations of the Baptist, Quaker, Free, and Christian Union churches filled out the religious world of this Erie Canal town.[10]

Ogdensburgh, a city of ten thousand persons in 1855, was located in the Town of Oswegatchie on the St. Lawrence River. A shipping center for the dairy farmers in the countryside, the city also contained a boat industry and railroad shops employing hundreds. Indirect evidence suggests that most of the workers were Irish immigrants. The city's frontier character had persisted from the 1790s until the 1840s when canal and railroad construction linked it to Boston, New York, and other markets in addition to its Montreal connection via the river. Ogdensburgh became a boom town in the 1850s. Occupational and ethnic diversity accompanied the changes that ironically brought the city into the mainstream of America. By 1855, Irish immigration raised Roman Catholic communicants to first

place among church members. Methodist Episcopal and Presbyterian congregations, each with four hundred, were the
largest Protestant denominations. Smaller churches were the
Unitarian, Baptist, Episcopalian, and Congregationalist, in
order of size. By 1850 the town's occupational structure included farmers, 25 percent; farm laborers, 20 percent; and artisans, tradesmen, and mechanics, 20 percent. White-collar
occupations came to about 15 percent. In politics St. Lawrence
County had long been Democratic, but despite the fact that
the widely known Barnburner and Free Soil Democratic leader
Preston King resided and maintained a law office there, the
city of Ogdensburgh supported the Whig party. No antislavery society or active corps of abolitionists could be found in
Ogdenburgh. New Hartford, on the other hand, was influenced by its proximity to Utica's abolition movement and by
the Finney revival movement. When the Kansas-Nebraska Act
was introduced, both small cities and their farming environs
joined the anti-extensionist protest movement by petitioning
Congress. Under King's leadership Ogdensburgh antislavery
Democrats and Whigs were early in opting for merger into a
new party.[11]

Our sample of 1,720 names was derived from an original
number of 4,057 anti–Nebraska Act and anti–Fugitive Slave
Law petitioners from these two areas as well as other New
York and Massachusetts towns. The anti–Nebraska Act memorials and petitions expressed the basic message in three
ways: against repeal of the Missouri Compromise of 1820, for
repeal of the Kansas-Nebraska Act, and for formation of a
new political party on a non-extensionist platform.

The largest petitions used in this study were sent to Congress from Lynn (870), Utica (755), and Fall River (690). Og-
densburgh-Oswegatchie names were gathered from two anti-
Nebraska Act petitions (56 and 66 signers) and from a printed
call for an anti–Nebraska Act party convention held in the
summer of 1854, signed by 185 men. A prominent role was
played by Springfield and Worcester citizens, but petitions from
these cities were relatively small (235 and 138 respectively).
The remainder of the names came from New Hartford, Rome,
and Schenectady. In the final sample 42 percent of all the

the late 1830s appears to be little changed. However, the increased ratio of skilled and unskilled among the petitioners does reflect a growing factory system in the early 1850s. Their 10 percent represented a rise from the 6.5 percent of only sixteen years earlier. The skilled men's ratio declined but they remained slightly higher than their group's share of the general occupational structure. Labor was clearly an important antislavery force, but the low representation of unskilled may point to a failure of communication between middle-class leaders and workers. This may reflect, too, the influence of nativism in alienating the foreign-born factory operatives and laborers. But even this source of cultural conflict may have been dissolving, as some birthplace and church data suggest.

Immigrants did append their names to anti–Kansas-Nebraska Act petitions (see Table 8–2). Of 1,440 men with known birthplaces (country or state) 322 were born outside of the United States, overwhelmingly in the British Isles. Notably, 110 Irish men signed petitions. They were 7.6 percent of the total. The Irish Catholics, in addition to poverty, experienced discrimination and clerical pressure to eschew secular social movements, especially those aimed against governmental authority. This subscription of their names indicates a crack in the wall of bigotry as well as their own adoption and assertion of American and republican identities. Of those 110 Irish petitioners occupations were found for 105, among whom 80 held manual labor jobs, 11 were farmers, and 14 were in white-collar positions. Half of the "blue-collar" men were in skilled occupations. Skilled English, Welsh, Scotch, and German-born men were in the majority in their respective nationalities among the signers. They too had been quick to claim the republican heritage and their citizenship in opposing the spread of slavery.

Available church membership information permits only an approximate portrait of the signers' religious communities and individual affiliations (see Table 8–3). The established Protestant monopoly had disappeared by 1854, but Presbyterians, Baptists, and Methodists dominate as they did in the 1830s. Catholics, one Jewish tailor from Poland, and a handful of Worcester's Free Church adherents introduce a semblance of

Table 8–2
Birthplaces of Petitioners, 1854–55

State or Nation	(N)	%
New York	555	39.5
Maine	15	1.0
Vermont	38	2.6
New Hampshire	41	2.8
Massachusetts	328	22.8
Connecticut	74	5.1
Rhode Island	49	3.4
New Jersey	5	.3
Pennsylvania	3	.2
Other States	10	.7
Total Native-born	1118	77.4
England	102	7.1
Scotland	31	2.2
Ireland	110	7.6
Wales	22	1.5
Canada	15	1.0
France	7	.5
Germany	32	2.2
Poland	1	.1
Other Countries	2	.1
Total Foreign-born	322	22.3

dissent and diversity. More conservative denominations such as the Dutch Reformed and Protestant Episcopal, linked as they were to men of property, indicate further the breadth of the anti–Kansas-Nebraska Act response. Of the Episcopalian signers, 55 percent were in white-collar groups. Of the Dutch Reformed signers, 44 percent were in those categories, with an equal portion in skilled jobs. Among Catholics, Presbyterians, Baptists, and Methodists, artisans were the largest group. Moreover, if there ever was any meaningful division of Prot-

Table 8–3
Church Affiliation of Petitioners, 1854–55

Church	(N)	%
Baptist	70	14.3
Free Church of Worcester	4	.8
Congregationalist	34	6.9
Methodist	88	18.0
Presbyterian	105	21.4
Dutch Reformed	30	6.1
Protestant Episcopal	58	11.8
Roman Catholic	60	12.2
Jewish	1	.2
Unitarian	23	4.7
Quaker	9	1.8
Universalist	4	.8
Christian	4	.8
Totals	490	99.8

Table 8–4
Assessed Value of Petitioners' Real Property, 1854–55

Amount	(N)	%
None	481	56.7
Less than $200	19	2.2
$201 to $500	178	21.0
$501 to $1,000	34	4.0
$1,001 to $5,000	95	11.2
$5,001 to $10,000	18	2.1
More than $10,000	24	2.8
Totals	849	100

estants between ritualists and pietists, the anti–Nebraska Act response appears to have eliminated it.

Anti–Nebraska Act petitioners embraced men on all levels of real property ownership, although, as Table 8–4 indicates, more than half of the petitioners for whom tax assessments were found—in Ogdensburgh, Fall River, Lynn and Worcester—were propertyless. The bulk of the remaining 43 percent owned from $201 to $500 of real property. These petitioners with relatively small holdings, together with the nonowners, suggest that anti–Nebraska Act petitioners included a large number of lower-class citizens.

The extent of home-ownership among occupational groups differed in three of the cities under study. In Lynn there was widespread home-ownership. A significant portion of men held real estate valued at between $1,001 and $5,000. In Worcester, however, men without real estate comprised 64 percent, and in their ranks skilled men had the highest rate of non-ownership (48 percent). In Fall River, where industrialization had become palpable in its famed mile of factories, the propertyless anti–Nebraska Act signers comprised 85 percent. The unskilled men's share ran second to that of the skilled. But some white-collar men (in the proprietor-manager-official group) ran a close third.

Among those in the tax records nonowners of personal property were also widespread, comprising 87 percent of the total (Table 8–5). In Lynn the figure was 76 percent, and most of this group were found to be skilled workers.

Table 8–5
Assessed Value of Petitioners' Personal Property, 1854–55

Amount	(N)	%
None	712	86.9
Less than $100	7	.9
$101 to $500	27	3.3
$501 to $1,000	30	3.7
$1,001 to $5,000	30	3.7
$5,001 to $10,000+	13	1.6
Totals	819	100

The wide dimensions of the anti–Nebraska Act constituency were evident in the social composition of the petitioners
and the crowds at mass meetings of protest. The presence of
immigrants among the public demonstrators introduced a new
component in the antislavery struggle. Indeed, in New York
City and Chicago, the German middle-class and radical artisans led the way. British-born anti–Nebraska Act men, including Catholic Irish men, were another new feature of the
movement. Together with the American-born in the industrial cities they helped to bring about a qualitative change in
this massive reform effort. Free Soilism had played a great
role in the transformation, but so did a growing popular de-
termination to limit the spread and accomplish the abolition
of slavery.

The Fugitive Slave Law, which was part of the Compromise
of 1850, proved to be a force for change even though the immediate response was ambivalent. Stanley W. Campbell, the
historian of that law, shows that Northerners, while abhor-
ring it, acquiesced in its passage. Only a minority led by abolitionists protested as the bill went through Congress and
was signed by President Millard Fillmore. Only a dedicated
few dared to obstruct enforcement of the law, which they denounced as immoral. Most Northerners, while hating the law,
abided it. Molders of public opinion such as "clergymen, busi-
nessmen, and industrialists in the larger cities, and politicians in Congress" won public support for the compromise.[13]
Abolitionists attempted many rescues of fugitives—sometimes with dramatic success, but often with failure. But public opinion could not for long ignore or be unsympathetic with
their ventures in defiance. By 1854 the passage of the Kansas-Nebraska Act helped decisively to turn public opinion
around.

The implications of that reversal are important to our ap-
preciation of the variable quality of racism. They make somewhat superficial and imprecise those historical interpreta-
tions that reduce Free Soilism and the 1854 upheavals to the
selfishness of whites seeking to preserve the territories for their
own opportunities. The anti–Nebraska Act movement grew
around several antislavery activities including the persis-

tence of militant black and white abolitionists who continued to defy United States marshals hunting down escaped blacks.[14]

There were many striking examples of citizens' sympathy for blacks in the increasingly strong and open disapproval of the Fugitive Slave Law. The Lynn voters' petition containing 870 signatures filed in the heat of the anti–Nebraska Act upsurge called for repeal of the law. If successful, the repeal would have permitted free movement of escaped slaves in the Northern states and in the territories. The petition begins with the signatures of the mayor, the aldermen, and city councilmen. Eight hundred and fifty voters then added theirs. This action appears to have been a united and deliberate expression of the citizens, quite like that of the many town meetings and city denunciations of the bill. Notably, the petition was signed on July 4, 1854. The Kansas-Nebraska Act had been the law since May, and on Independence Day it seemed unlikely that it would be repealed. The petition appears to have been an effort to retain the momentum of protest against the spread of slavery and the continued repression of blacks.

The change in opinion between 1846, when the Wilmot Proviso was first proposed, and the anti–Nebraska Act protest of 1854 centered on non-extensionism but did not jettison basic radical abolitionism. The change in opinion could be seen, too, in the emergence of the Republican party, with platforms embodying 1830s abolition demands.[15]

Another example of this growing opposition was revealed in the Northern Cotton Whig, Amos A. Lawrence. He had been unyielding and unforgiving of antislavery Whigs into the early 1850s in his desire to maintain harmonious political and business relations with Southern planters. Lawrence had also upheld the 1850 Compromise although initially he supported Massachusetts' unwillingness to assist the slave hunters. He had caved in to slave hunting when Thomas Simms, a black waiter in Boston, was marched under armed guard to a vessel waiting to transport him to the South and slavery. In this instance Lawrence volunteered to assist the United States marshal. But in May 1854 when Anthony Burns was seized by marshals, Lawrence led other conservatives in offering to provide the legal talent to defend Burns. Lawrence angrily denounced the capture of this black man. Clearly he was also hitting back at Senator Stephen A. Douglas's destabilizing bill. But, like the "commercial class" of Boston, he had taken "a new position on the great question of the day."[16]

Some historians probably have magnified the white selfishness in the Free Soil movement. The fugitive slave issue illuminated the large part that more disinterested impulses played. That lord of the loom, Amos A. Lawrence, was forced to subordinate his business interests to those of the commonwealth. "You may rest upon it," he wrote, "that the sentiment at this time among the powerful and conservative class of men is the same as it is in the country towns throughout New England."[17] The "powerful class" had rediscovered the sources of republican strength as Birney, Whittier, Weld, Goodell, Nathan P. Rogers, the Stantons, Grimkes, and Lovejoys had discovered them in the 1830s and 1840s. The source of republican virtue in the 1850s remained in the antislavery rank and file.[18]

NOTES

1. William W. Rice,"Worcester County in the Free Soil Movement," in D. Hamilton Hurd, *History of Worcester County* (Philadelphia, 1889), pp. 1658–69; James Eugene Mooney, "Antislavery in Worcester County: A Case Study" (Ph.D. dissertation, Clark University, 1971), pp. 152–53; David Donald, *Charles Sumner and the Rights of Man* (New York: Knopf, 1970), vol. 1, p. 177; Paul Goodman, "Politics of Industrialism: Massachusetts, 1830–1870," in Richard L. Bushman, ed., *Uprooted Americans: Essays to Honor Oscar Handlin* (Boston: Little, Brown, 1979), pp. 184–87; *Utica Morning Herald*, November 9, 1848; Alan Dawley, *Class and Community: The Industrial Revolution in Lynn* (Cambridge: Harvard University Press, 1976), p. 65.

2. Goodman, "Politics of Industrialism," p. 189.

3. Edward Magdol, *Owen Lovejoy: Abolitionist in Congress* (New Brunswick: Rutgers University Press, 1967), p. 89.

4. *New York Times*, January–March, 1854; *Springfield Republican*, February 16 to March 10, 1854; (Worcester) *Massachusetts Spy*, March 1–22, April 26, 1854; Bruce Levine, "Immigrants, Class, and Politics: The Germans of New York and the Kansas-Nebraska Act of

1854" (Unpublished paper, Graduate Center, City of University of New York, 1979); Karl Obermann, *Joseph Weydemeyer, Pioneer of American Socialism* (New York: International Publishers, 1947), pp. 78–80.

5. "The Proceedings of a Mass Meeting of several Thousand Mechanics, Workingmen and other citizens of New York remonstrating against the repeal of the Missouri Compromise," February 20, 1854, Joseph Simpson, president, National Archives, RG 233, H33–G24.4; Dr. Thomas D. Andrews, Home Corresponding Secretary, Society of Universal Democratic Republicanism, to House of Representatives (Referred to House Committee on Territories, April 3, 1854), National Archives, RG 233, HR33A–G24.2, LC Collection, Box 157.

6. March 11, 1854, Matthew Bell and 71 other workingmen, Eagle Foundry, Albany, New York, to House of Representatives, National Archives, RG 233, HR33A–G24.2.

7. Haverhill annual town meeting resolution, March 1854, National Archives, RG 233, HR33A–H1.19, LC Collection, Box 156; Mooney, "Antislavery in Worcester County," pp. 216–17; John G. Metcalf, *Annals of the Town of Mendon* (Providence, 1880), pp. 622–23; *Massachusetts Spy*, February 15, and March 15, 1854. Reverend Higginson and his Free Church flock deserve attention. He had been attracted to this minister's post in Worcester because he had found "as much radicalism . . . as at Lynn but more varied, more cultivated, and more balanced by an opposing force." His flock he called "Jerusalem wildcats" and "intelligent mechanics." Among his associates in a daring attempt to rescue the fugitive Anthony Burns was John C. Cluer, ex-Chartist, agent of the state antislavery society and ten-hour advocate. Higginson had endangered his security in a Newburyport church in 1852 when he publicly supported striking workers in Amesbury. See Tilden G. Edelstein, *Strange Enthusiasm: A Life of Thomas Wentworth Higginson* (New Haven: Yale University Press, 1968), pp. 135–36, and Mary Thacher Higginson, *Thomas Wentworth Higginson, The Story of His Life* (Boston, 1914), pp. 115–16.

8. *Massachusetts Spy*, March 15, 1854.

9. *Proceedings of a Public Meeting of Citizens of Providence, . . . March 7, 1854, to Protest against Slavery in Nebraska* (Providence, 1854); Quarterly Meeting, Free Will Baptists, Western, R.I., March 2, 1854 petition to House of Representatives, National Archives, RG 233.

10. Manuscript United States Census, 1850, and manuscript New York State Census, 1855.

11. Ibid.; Harry F. Landon, *The North Country. A History Embracing Jefferson, St. Lawrence* [and other] *counties, New York,* 3 vols. (Indianapolis, 1932); Curtis Gates, ed., *Our County and Its People: A Memorial Record of St. Lawrence County* (Syracuse, 1894); P. S. Garand, *The History of the City of Ogdensburgh* (Ogdensburgh, 1927); Ernest Paul Miller, "Preston King, A Political Biography" (Ph.D. dissertation, Columbia University, 1957); Judah B. Ginsberg, "Barnburners, Free Soilers and the New York Republican Party," *New York History* 57 (October 1976); 475–500.

12. See note 1, chapter 5 above.

13. Stanley W. Campbell, *The Slave Catchers: Enforcement of the Fugitive Slave Law, 1850–1860* (New York: Norton Library, 1970; originally Chapel Hill: University of North Carolina Press, 1968), p. 66.

14. On the weakness of the argument that Negrophobia determined Free Soilism and the growth of Republicanism see John M. Rozett, "Racism and Republican Emergence in Illinois, 1848–1860: A Re-evaluation of Republican Negrophobia," *Civil War History* 22 (1976): 101–15.

15. One example of this radical abolitionist influence in the fledgling People's and Republican parties in 1854 is the set of resolutions adopted by the Massachusetts State Republican party convention, July 1854. It includes one on abolition of slavery in the District of Columbia and the Territories and on the prohibition of admitting slave states to the Union and of acquiring potential slaveholding territory. *Massachusetts Spy*, July 26, 1854.

16. Thomas H. O'Connor, *Lords of the Loom: The Cotton Whigs and the Coming of the Civil War* (New York: Charles Scribner's Sons, 1968), pp. 96–101.

17. Ibid., p. 101.

18. At the time of his death, Edward Magdol was preparing an addition to this chapter in which he would relate his work to the views of other antebellum historians. His notes on Michael F. Holt, for example, take issue with Holt's views that in the 1850s local concerns were of greater importance than the national issue of slavery, and that the crisis in the two-party system did not emerge until that same decade. (Michael F. Holt, *The Political Crisis of the 1850s* New York: John Wiley and Sons, 1978.) E. M.'s view was that the crisis of the party system manifested itself as early as the mid-1840s and was related to the defections over the issue of the extension of slavery, "indeed, over party silence over slavery in both Whig and Democratic parties." He went on to note that "working-class atti-

tudes were already expressed as: rid us of both wrongs—wage and chattel slavery."

On a different matter, E. M. was planning to amplify on his remark that "historians probably have magnified the white-selfishness in the free soil movement." He saw the Free Soil party as ambivalent about racial equality, but emphasized that the attitude toward blacks was "a dynamic process, not a static condition." Some in the Free Soil movement clearly were racist, while others helped to repeal some of the black laws. (James M. McPherson, *Ordeal by Fire: The Civil War and Reconstruction* New York: Alfred A. Knopf, 1982.)

Richard Sewell also describes the Free Soilers' ambivalence toward blacks, but says they bucked the racist current by their anti-extensionism and their opposition to black laws and the Fugitive Slave Law. (Richard H. Sewell, *Ballots for Freedom: Antislavery Politics in the United States, 1837–1860* New York: Oxford University Press, 1976, chap. 8, passim.)

Further evidence of the variable attitude toward racism appears among the members of the new Republican party. Eric Foner says that even though some members revealed racist sentiments, generally "their actions in state legislatures and in Congress" demonstrated their support of equal rights for blacks. (Eric Foner, *Free Soil, Free Labor, Free Men* London: Oxford University Press, 1970, pp. 281–295, passim.)

CHAPTER 9

Conclusions

This journey to the social roots of the abolitionist movement has yielded a portrait of an ever widening constituency. The movement grew during America's early industrialization and was shaped by a consensus of republicanism. As republican values and principles pointed to equal economic and social opportunity, so their adherents aspired to improvements in their own lives and in the lives of others. George Henry Evans's slogan "vote yourself a farm" and the Homestead movement were the traditional and political expressions of that republican concern among laborers, farmers, and many middle-class Americans.[1] Orestes Brownson offered a sharper version of labor's viewpoint: "We have no toleration for either system [of labor: "free" or slave]. We would see the slave a man, but a free man, not a mere operative at wages."[2] His statement appears to have been a concise modernization of equal rights goals for the 1830s.

Men of growing wealth, property, and political power also steered by a republican star. For them, republicanism held out the promise of enrichment, economic independence, markets, and property accumulation in a competitive political system. The possessive individualism that informed their conduct did not at first exclude concerns for the commonwealth.

A republic of competing "buyers" and "sellers", producers and consumers, fit nicely into a marketplace analogy. There was no room in it in the 1830s for economic or political monopolies and aristocratic privileges.

Manufacturing capitalists and journeymen in the dawn of American industrialism may have shared an antiaristocratic world view, but by the mid-1830s the gulf between their real interests was beginning to widen. By the mid-1840s and the 1850s factory laborers and craftsmen frequently denounced a new aristocracy of industrial capitalists. The "free labor" concept became a rhetorical vestige of millowner ideology and hegemony. But among skilled workingmen and small workshop owners it retained its original content and significance. Brownson once again furnished a trenchant criticism. He charged that both slavery and wage labor prevented a worker from becoming "an independent laborer on his own capital—on his own farm or in his own shop."[3] "Free labor" continued to be an optimistic notion nourishing the producer's republicanism, which in turn predisposed laboring and middle-class groups toward abolitionism and free speech. In that connection, the veteran abolitionist Wendell Phillips recalled during the Civil War that the antislavery agitation saved the republic. "The agitation," Phillips wrote, "was commenced when the Declaration of Independence was signed."[4] And striking Lynn shoe workers in 1860 sang a song that made that document's ideals come alive in the orbit of their own class experience:

> Resolve by your native soil
>   Resolve by your fathers' graves
> You will live by your honest toil,
>   But never consent to be slaves![5]

Other inspirations besides those generated directly by changing workplace relations brought men and women to protest against slavery. The powerful pietistic-perfectionist tradition also shaped the abolitionist quest for regeneration and moral order. Those who regarded the world as a place in moral and material decline, but still capable of salvation and perfection, advanced utopian notions alongside specific reform measures. The Second Great Awakening that surged from below in 1800 inspired the poor, the uneducated, the laboring population to demand democratic reform in the churches. Drawing upon the egalitarian ideals of the English and American revolutions, upstart mechanic theologians on both sides of the English-speaking Atlantic world led this "levelling" process. Upper-class clergymen feared that "tinkers and taylors, weavers, shoemakers and country mechanics of all kinds" had gained control of the churches.[6] Methodists, Baptists, and the Christian Disciples churches were the religious workingmen's preferred sanctuaries in this process, and it was no accident that they played leading roles in antislavery protest. The republican ideal of equality stimulated nonconformist English artisans and American lower orders in church democratization and abolitionism. Finally, large numbers of nonchurch men kept alive the popular deism that had flourished briefly in the post-Revolutionary era. Its rationalist temper also predisposed them toward abolition, Free Soil, and political republicanism.

For their part, abolitionists accepted Free Soilism as a step toward the "ultimate extinction" of slavery. They learned too that its attractive power enlarged their constituency. By the 1850s the native-born antislavery rank and file was augmented by foreign-born men rapidly absorbing republican values in assimilating into American politics and society. Moreover, that widening and growing coalition displaced the distracting and transitory nativism of Know-Nothingism even as it postponed a final reckoning with white supremacy. Slavery was perceived as the main danger to the republic; for a third of a century men and women were mobilized by abolitionism and Free Soilism. The movement was diverted from a cul-de-sac of purist-perfectionism into a somewhat unruly and flawed but powerful political torrent.

Much empirical research needs to be done in order to complete the portrait of the national antislavery constituency. This study represents only one section, the industrializing Northeast. Other sections in which abolitionism was influential require study. Who were the petitioners, antislavery society members, and voters of Liberty, Free Soil, and Republican parties in Ohio, eastern Tennessee, Indiana, Illinois and other

Northwest Ordinance states and territories? Who was in the antislavery ranks in frontier or recently settled communities? How did they differ from Northeasterners? Are there similarities or differences between antislavery rank and file in industrializing Pittsburgh, Newark, Cincinnati, Milwaukee, Chicago, or Rochester, New York, and the boot, shoe, and textile producing New England and New York cities?

How did pietism-perfectionism, secular radicalism, republicanism, and industrialization combine to shape and move the antislavery rank and file west and south of New York and Massachusetts? How did families, classes, churches, and ethnicity in other areas affect the antislavery movement? Finally, is the legacy of abolitionism discernible in post-emancipation institutions and communities?

By posing these questions we have only begun to examine antislavery as a feature of changing society. We have partially answered some questions by rediscovering some of the antislavery petitioners. Thanks are tendered to the agitators and circulators, and the later archivists and historians. And of course, thanks to the carpenters, shoemakers, cotton mill laborers, machinists, grocers, manufacturers, editors, clergymen, and housewives, and others in their numbers.

NOTES

1. Helene Zahler, *Eastern Workingmen and Public Land Policy* (New York: Columbia University Press, 1941); Edward Pessen, *Most Uncommon Jacksonians: The Radical Leaders of the Early Labor Movement* (Albany: State University of New York Press, 1967), p. 72.

2. Orestes Brownson, "The Laboring Classes," cited in Edwin C. Rozwenc, ed., *Ideology and Power in the Age of Jackson* (New York: Anchor Books, 1964), p. 325.

3. Ibid., p. 328.

4. The source of this quote could not be found. (M.S.M. and M.G.)

5. Alonzo Lewis, "Cordwainers' Song," cited in Alan Dawley, *Class and Community: The Industrial Revolution in Lynn, Massachusetts, 1780–1860* (Albany: State University of New York Press, 1981), pp. 82–83.

6. Nathan O. Hatch, "The Christian Movement and the Demand for a Theology of the People," *Journal of American History* 67 (De-

cember 1980): 567; Seymour Drescher, "Two Variants of Anti-Slavery: Religious Organization and Social Mobilization in Britain and France," in Drescher and Christine Bolt, eds., *Anti-Slavery, Religion and Reform* (Hamden, Conn.: Dawson-Archon, 1980), p. 43; Drescher, "Cart Whip and Billy Roller: Or Antislavery and Reform Symbolism in Industrializing Britain," *Journal of Social History* 15 (Fall 1981): 3–24.

Notes on Past Scholarship Toward the Antislavery Profile

During the 1960s historians began to reverse the image of the abolitionist leaders, who had been seen as misfits, out of step with their times. Louis Filler led off with his modern history of the movement, in which abolitionists were portrayed as sincere reformers who facilitated a revolution in human rights. Their work became important because of their "consistency and dedication." Betty Fladeland refuted myths that abolitionists were neurotic, abnormal zealots. She demonstrated that they were like their fellow citizens, sharing their experiences, aspirations, and expectations. And in a volume of essays edited by Martin Duberman, abolitionists were seen as responsible defenders of freedom.[1] A new generation's positive and sympathetic appraisal of the movement was further reinforced in the 1960s and 1970s by book-length biographies of abolitionist personalities.[2] Although the earlier negative descriptions remained acceptable to some historians, others were not satisfied with them. David Donald's 1956 essay, analyzing 106 New England abolitionist leaders of the 1830s, found them to be young men and women alienated from the "new industrial society." By turning their energies to reform, and especially to abolitionism, Donald asserted, they made a "quite unconscious attack upon the new industrial system." Donald argued that these sons and daughters of displaced and superceded Federalist and mercantile elites flocked to abolitionism in order to retrieve lost social standing. Donald's essay attempted an empirical test of Avery Craven's earlier contention that abolitionism was a product of industrial, agricultural, and cultural changes. Donald's linkage of status anxiety concepts to the emergence of industrial capitalism and to ideas of immediate abolitionism placed the discussion in a more coherent reality.

A scholarly debate ensued between Donald and his critics. Gerald Sorin found that New York State abolitionist leaders were men of substantial means and attainments who did not suffer a loss of status. Soon, Leonard Richards offered a more substantial rebuttal of the Donald thesis. Analyzing anti-abolitionist mob violence in the Jackson era, Richards found that the older elites in Utica and Cincinnati turned sharply against abolitionism rather than toward it in order to protect their hegemony. Abolitionists in those cities tended to be rising manufacturers, artisans, men with a stake in a "free labor" society not afraid to disturb the national detente between the slave South and the Northern system. Richards came close to giving us a social portrait of the rank and file antislavery men. James B. Stewart's lively history of the movement accepted the notion of a middle-class and farmer movement. In the end, much had been learned of the abolitionist leadership, particularly through Richard's novel study of mob actions. In addition, an inkling of knowledge had been gained about the breadth of antislavery support.[3]

Other studies continued to explore the antislavery social profile. In a small-scale investigation of Worcester County, Massachusetts, antislavery activity, James Mooney revealed the prominence of farmer and artisan names in one document. This helped to persuade him that the abolitionists appealed to the "common people." In a much larger sampling of Jackson era workingmen in New York City, John Jentz showed that their roots in radical republicanism prepared them for their numerically significant participation in antislavery petitioning. My own study of three cities in New York and one in Massachusetts produced a preliminary social profile of 677 antislavery petitioners. They appeared to be composed largely of middle-class merchants and professionals, journeyman craftsmen, and masters-cum-manufacturers. They seemed to be inspired by democratic republican and antimonopolistic ideals prevalent in the Jackson period. They also displayed the effects of liberal Protestantism. My earlier pilot study of anti-Nebraska Act petitioners in the lake port and rail terminus of Ogdensburgh, New York, and in Utica's Fifth Ward caught the movement after a generation of agitation and political action. This latter constituency proved to be similar to the earlier one but with more laborers and foreign-born men, and even some Irish Catholic men apparently ignoring clerical caveats against taking part in secular antiestablishment demonstrations.[4]

Studies of leadership have the advantage of recourse to literary sources such as letters, diaries, journals, and newspapers. Donald's and Sorin's collective biographical studies relied on such materials as well as on some quantitative evidence. A different approach is required if we are to find at least some of the hundreds in the ranks of the reform movement. With all due respect to the Beautiful Quintessential Single Example, I have also come to appreciate the necessity of numbers in social history. There are, of course, other techniques for unlocking the doors to histories of social groups and social movements. One of the boldest and most creative was George Rudé's study of the French revolutionary crowd, a method adopted by Richards in examining American mob actions. Jackson era violence provided a rich context for his probes of anti-abolitionist behavior which led him to their opposites and to new visions of early industrial capitalist society in America. Jentz and I adopted a variant of this method in utilizing antislavery petitions as the primary sources for quantification, linkage to social data, and reorganization into social profiles. From these we also inferred the intellectual stimuli of the antislavery rank and file. As the pages of this book have shown, the social historian receives an invitation to speculation that she or he cannot turn down. Linkage was used effectively by Judith Wellman, who relied on antislavery petitions to give her a constituency in upstate New York's "burned-over district." Wellman studied the links between dedicated antislavery men and women and religious enthusiasm. Later, Wellman elucidated the roles of women in antislavery agitation and organization, as well as in their churches, from the petitions and linkage to cultural and social data.[5]

Earlier applications of the technique had been attempted by David Brion Davis in his sweeping work on antislavery thought in America, England, and France during the revolutionary period from 1770 to 1823. Quaker "men of wealth, influence, and power" dominated the lists of members in the Pennsylvania Abolition Society and the New York Manumission Society. In the latter they were also "the 'high command' of the Federalist party." They included such men as Alexander Hamilton and John Jay. This elite group was composed of merchants, bankers, and lawyers. Davis also found small numbers of skilled workingmen and tradesmen in the Pennsylvania organization. However, its committees were dominated by men in high political office, and by doctors, lawyers, and merchants. They seem to have been a coterie of upper-class republicanism, imbued with the values of virtue and commerce that distinguished them from English counterparts such as Wilberforce and Clarkson. Although Davis's studies were on a modest scale, they pointed the way to a full-blown reconstruction of the early republic's antislavery leadership and membership.[6]

Two historians recently have attempted to describe and analyze the abolitionist Liberty party's political constituency during the 1840s. Allan M. Kraut investigated western New York State and Reinhard O. Johnson concentrated his study on Massachusetts and New Hampshire voting patterns.[7]

Johnson uncovered a Liberty party tendency to be stronger in manufacturing towns than in other Massachusetts communities. In New Hampshire the Liberty party led the way by entering coalitions, first with the Whigs or National Republicans, and, later in the decade, with the Democrats. By 1847 a Liberty–Independent Democratic alliance made gains in the Democratic "frontier regions or poorer mountainous areas" of the Granite State. The densely populated southeastern commercial towns were influenced by Liberty party presses in Amesbury and Boston, and by Massachusetts Liberty party speakers such as John G. Whittier and Henry B. Stanton. Those New Hampshire communities soon became Liberty party strongholds.

The changing composition of the state's Liberty party is evident in Johnson's findings on partisan politics. From a largely ex-Whig organization the party turned increasingly into an ex-Democrat or Independent Democratic one. The fight over the annexation of Texas in 1844 fed this transformation. At the same time, the Democratic leadership, sensing the sharp change in voter attitudes to a position against the extension of slavery, seized the issue from the Liberty men and captured the state legislature and governor's office in the 1847 election. The opportunism of the famed Isaac Hill Democratic machine is evident. So too is the effect of abolitionist agitation of their "Bible politics." Curiously they came together to answer the needs of an electorate of modest means that was eager to preserve democratic society.

Kraut's analysis of the Liberty rank and file in sixty-four western New York towns yielded a profile of that constituency. It was composd of white males, largely in their thirties, most of whom were native to the state. They frequently were small merchants, tradesmen, and farmers, and they were generally poorer than their neighbors. They showed a mild tendency to belong to pietistic churches. In a subsequent study of 182 men in the poll lists of Smithfield in 1841 and 1845, Kraut located 88 who were linked to other data. He found that 55 were Liberty men. Although he determined that 33 were not members of the Liberty party he was unable to discover whether they belonged to other parties. Kraut distinguished Liberty and non-Liberty men by the terms "abolitionists" and "nonabolitionist." Artisans were well represented in both groups. "Laborers" made up 26.7 percent of the abolitionists and only 10 percent of the nonabolitionists. Professionals tended to be outside of the Liberty party; migrants from New England were more likely to be Liberty voters.

Kraut also used a Smithfield subscriber list for an antislavery newspaper to identify these men. Farmers constituted the largest occupational group among the readers. They were somewhat underrepresented, for their 61.5 percent showing in the list fell below the western New York farming population of 75 percent. On the other hand, the "town" constituency was overrepresented. Artisans, local merchants, and one laborer comprised almost 40 percent of the subscribers' list at a time when "nonfarming 'bone and muscle' occupations" were only 25 percent of the state's work force. The self-styled "Poor Man's Party" appeared to be increasingly successful in appealing to lower-class and some middle-class men. We may infer from the work of Johnson and Kraut that these white men were gaining the conviction that the enslavement of black men was of consequence to them. The species of "slavery" that they perceived in New York and New England probably elicited their sympathy for the Southern slave while it increased consciousness of their self-interest. The Liberty message that chattel slavery endangered a free labor society appears to have struck responsive nerves. The small departures from the two-party system in New Hampshire, New York, and Massachusetts index that larger political trend and shed new light on the texture of the growing antislavery political constituency. The portrait of the rank and file in the Liberty decade remains to be completed in these as well as in other Northeastern states, in Pennsylvania, and in the states of the Old Northwest.

The social composition of the women among the rank and file abolitionists is just beginning to emerge. Some features of the group's leadership have been described recently in biographies of the Grimke sisters, Elizabeth Cady Stanton, Abby Kelley Foster, Lydia Maria Child, Sojourner Truth, and Frances Ellen Watkins. From Maine to Michigan these women brought hundreds of others into female antislavery societies which plunged into petition campaigns with tremendous energy and resolve. These women's actions also served as large-scale political demonstrations against their exclusion from citizenship and from recognized social equality. Women assumed the leading roles in local antislavery education, agitation, and fund raising. They also participated effectively in national-level organization.[8]

The roles of rank and file women have become better known

through the more recent studies of Wellman, Henle and Heard, and Lerner. Wellman's studies of northern and western New York female abolitionists have pioneered in describing and analyzing their activities. Ellen Henle and Patricia Heard have advanced our knowledge of both female and male petitioners in their work on Sandwich, New Hampshire. Gerda Lerner's research reveals the role of families in abolition activity and emphasizes women's political consciousness.[9]

Wellman has uncovered a striking feature of the movement's social composition. In one town she found a proportion of factory worker involvement much larger than in any other place studied by any other historian. Thirty-four townships which were represented in the 1838–39 petitions were those in which "manufacturing and trade" was slightly greater than in towns regarded as agricultural and which Wellman calls "nonabolitionist." In the former, agriculture claimed 70 percent of the employed, and "manufacturing and trade," 23.2 percent. In "nonabolitionist" towns, agriculture claimed 76.7 percent, and manufacturing and trade, 16.6 percent. The women's occupations are not known but their religious affiliations are. More women petitioners probably were members of Baptist, Methodist, Quaker, and Presbyterian churches than of Episcopal, Catholic, Dutch Reformed, and Universalist-Unitarian. This is inferred by Wellman from the more sympathetic attitudes of the first group toward women's antislavery activities.

A rare glimpse of worker support of abolitionists is provided in Wellman's study of the petitions of Paris Township, New York. This group of early mill settlements, but ten miles away from Utica, had a predominantly native-born population of approximately twenty-eight hundred in 1840. Over the period of ten years between 1835 and 1845 it generated fifteen petitions signed by both men and women. This number is about three times as many as in other towns of comparable size in the region. Paris grew rapidly in the 1830s. Due to the introduction of two textile factories which employed many women, the population of adult women grew rapidly, rising to 53 percent of the population by 1835. Whether or not these working women were antislavery petitioners has not yet been determined. Wellman used the occupations of some of the married women's husbands to give an indication of the women signers' social standing. About 39 percent of the forty-eight women for whom such information was available were the wives of farmers. About 23 percent of the husbands were factory workers, and 17 percent were artisans. The tendency of families to participate in antislavery activities may not be illustrated in this case. However, it does permit another valuable guess: that among the petitioners were impressive numbers of factory operatives. The information provided by Wellman offers indirect evidence of factory worker involvement, although the absence of factory records prevents its confirmation.

Further evidence of abolition's appeal to men and women of modest means and middle- and lower-class standing is provided by Heard and Henle's analysis of Sandwich, New Hampshire, petitioners. This was a relatively stable town in the midst of farming country. Of the 260 female signers, 116 were identified by their church affiliation and by their marital status. They tended to be closely divided among Congregationalists, Quakers, Free Will Baptists, and Methodists. The social standing of the 222 men signers is indicated in their relatively low average tax payments. These were only slightly higher than those of non-signers. As Heard concludes, there appears to have been some appeal to "the man behind the plough" in this moral and rural New England village. The women antislavery petitioners are still only skimpily defined, but a comparison of male and female names indicates that they were not isolated individuals but members of families that signed petitions together. They appear to have been of that celebrated "middling" sort, neither rich nor poor productive toilers.

Impressive confirmation of family activity is provided by Gerda Lerner's research of female petitioners. Summarizing her own probe of Ohio female petitioners and the studies of New Hampshire and upstate New York women discussed above, Lerner concluded that abolitionism was advanced "to a large extent" by family groups. Women at first seemed to have followed their men's leads and urgings to sign petitions. But women, rapidly becoming conscious of their second-class standing, just as rapidly made abolitionism one of their moral concerns and a medium of practical political struggle to achieve equality. Their impact is evident in Oneida County, where women provided 70 percent of the petition signatures, and in Sandwich, where women outnumbered the men signers. That leading role is further emphasized in Lerner's research by the women who provided twice as many petition signatures as men on the 402 memorials sent to Congress from Northern states in 1837–38.

The first outlines of an abolitionist rank and file began to emerge from the studies noted above. If we may judge by their occupations and property status, they are masses of women and men in the lower and middle ranks of American society. The men are in their thirties and forties, and working-class and business-class men appeared to share a faith in the "free labor" ideology, which promised progress and economic independence. These petitioners were white and predominantly native-born Americans. New England birthplaces dominated the Massachusetts petitioners and were prominent among the New York signers. The male petitioners tended to belong to churches variously labeled "pietistic," "evangelical," or "low." Their opponents tended to belong to "ritualistic," or "non-evangelical," or "high" churches, suggesting a cultural component of their social class differences. However, as we have seen in this study, some blurring of these lines appeared in other places where antislavery activity occurred. Apart from the tiny minority of Liberty party enthusiasts, earlier studies revealed virtually nothing of the antislavery constituency's political ideals or party preferences. Antislavery activists appeared to reflect the dominant economic life in their communities: poorer farmers in Smithfield, New York, and middling farmers in Sandwich; skilled workingmen in New England manufacturing towns and in cities such as New York, Utica, and Fall River; possibly women mill operatives in a textile town like Paris, New York.

The men, and some of the women, who make up this rough profile of the rank and file of abolitionism and its supporters strongly resemble those whom antislavery leaders claimed for the backbone of their constituency. They were the "bone and muscle" of society, a rather proud formulation of the Jackson era's exaltation of the honest producer. James G. Birney, the corresponding secretary of the American Anti-Slavery Society and first Liberty party presidential candidate, looked for support among "the warm hearts of our yeomanry, and . . . the artisans and inhabitants of the smaller villages." Thomas Wentworth Higginson, another prominent abolitionist, recalled in his old age that the movement in New England reached more of those "in the factories and shoe shops" than in the pulpit, the bench and bar, or the halls of academe. William Goodell, then an organizer of abolition societies, exulted after the founding conventions of Worcester County organizations in the winter of 1836: "No! There was no haughty aristocracy upon the hills of Worcester county to tell the hardy lords of the soil that it was unconstitutional of them to buffet their native snowdrifts for the purpose of discussing the inalienable rights of man to freedom!" Thomas W. Ward II, a Shrewsbury, Massachusetts, abolitionist of the family that gave a Revolutionary War general to the fight for independence, put the approving stamp of New England's dissenting tradition on the movement. "Shall we the professed friends of liberty," he wrote, "descendants of the Pilgrim fathers—shall we whose fathers freed themselves from the bondage of foreign powers, stand back, and off our hands from this our native foe?"[10]

Taken together, these statements offered a preliminary impression of the antislavery constituency. They invited verification of the contemporary portrait of the nineteenth century's most compelling reform movement. They also prompted this inquiry into the relationship among the participants in that endeavor and the changing world of which they were a part.

This book was built on the works already cited, and goes beyond them to explore the abolitionist rank and file in some of the manufacturing cities of New York and Massachusetts. It identifies men and women who joined abolition societies, subscribed to their newspapers, signed petitions, and eventually voted for a succession of antislavery political parties. A reconstruction of the abolitionist movement in terms of its constituents furnishes some of the answers relevant to the history of reform and of industrialization, and of American society as a whole.

NOTES

1. Louis Filler, *The Crusade Against Slavery, 1830–1860* (New York: Harper and Row, 1960); Betty Fladeland, "Who Were the Abolitionists?" *Journal of Negro History* 43 (April 1964), 99–115; Martin Duberman, ed., *The Antislavery Vanguard: New Essays on the Abolitionists* (Princeton: Princeton University Press, 1965).

2. In addition to the biographies of women abolitionists noted below (note 8), some meriting consideration are Merton L. Dillon, *Elijah P. Lovejoy: Abolitionist Editor* (Urbana: University of Illinois Press, 1961), and *Benjamin Lundy and the Struggle for Negro Freedom* (Urbana: University of Illinois Press, 1966); John L. Thomas, *The Liberator, William Lloyd Garrison: A Biography* (Boston: Little, Brown, 1963); Walter M. Merrill, *Against Wind and Tide: A Biography of William Lloyd Garrison* (Cambridge: Harvard University Press, 1963); Richard H. Sewell, *John P. Hale and the Politics of Abolition* (Cambridge: Harvard University Press, 1965); Edward Magdol, *Owen Lovejoy, Abolitionist in Congress* (New Brunswick: Rutgers University Press, 1967); Tilden L. Edelstein, *Strange Enthusiasm: A Life of Thomas Wentworth Higginson* (New Haven: Yale University Press, 1968); Bertram Wyatt-Brown, *Lewis Tappan and the Evangelical War Against Slavery* (Cleveland: Press of Case Western Reserve University, 1969); James B. Stewart, *Joshua R. Giddings and the Tactics of Radical Politics* (Cleveland: Press of Case Western Reserve University, 1970); Patrick Riddleburger, *George Washington Julian, Radical Republican* (Indianapolis: Bobbs-Merrill, 1969).

3. David Donald, "Toward a Reconsideration of the Abolitionists" in *Lincoln Reconsidered* (New York: Alfred A. Knopf, 1956); Gerald Sorin, *The New York Abolitionists* (Westport, Conn.: Greenwood Press, 1970); Leonard L. Richards, *"Gentlemen of Property and Standing", Anti-abolition Mobs in Jacksonian America* (New York: Oxford University Press, 1970), chap. 5, pp. 131–155.

4. James Eugene Mooney, "Antislavery in Worcester County: A Case Study" (Ph.D. dissertation, Clark University, 1971); John Jentz, "The Antislavery Constituency in Jacksonian New York City," *Civil War History* 27 (June 1981): 101–122; Edward Magdol, "A Window on the Abolitionist Constituency: Antislavery Petitions, 1836–1839," in Alan M. Kraut, ed., *Crusaders and Compromisers: Essays on the*

Relationship of the Antislavery Struggle to the Ante Bellum Party System (Westport, Conn., Greenwood Press, 1983); Magdol, "A Remonstrance Against the Nebraska Bill, 1854: The Case of Ogdensburgh, New York, Antislavery Petitioners" (Paper presented at the Annual Meeting of the Organization of American Historians, April 13, 1978).

5. George Rudé, *The Crowd in the French Revolution* (New York: Oxford University Press, 1959); Judith Wellman, "The Burned-Over District Revisited: Benevolent Reform and Abolitionism in Mexico, Paris, and Ithaca, New York, 1825–1842" (Ph.D. dissertation, University of Virginia, 1974).

6. David Brion Davis, *The Problem of Slavery in the Age of Revolution* (Ithaca: Cornell University Press, 1975), p. 239.

7. Alan M. Kraut, "The Liberty Men of New York: Political Abolitionism in New York State, 1840–1848" (Ph.D. dissertation, Cornell University, 1975); Reinhard O. Johnson, "The Liberty Party in New England, 1840–1848: The Forgotten Abolitionists" (Ph.D. dissertation, Syracuse University, 1976); see also Kraut, "The Forgotten Reformers, A Profile of Third Party Abolitionists in Antebellum New York," in Lewis Perry and Michael Fellman, eds., *Antislavery Reconsidered: New Perspectives on the Abolitionists* (Baton Rouge: Louisiana State University Press, 1979); Johnson, "The Liberty Party in Massachustts, 1840–1848: Antislavery Third Party Politics in the Bay State," *Civil War History* 28 (September 1982): 237–265; Johnson, "The Liberty Party in New Hampshire, 1840–1848: Antislavery Politics in the Granite State," *Historical New Hampshire* 33 (Summer 1978): 123–165.

8. Gerda Lerner, *The Grimke Sisters from South Carolina: Rebels Against Slavery* (Boston: Little, Brown, 1967); Milton Meltzer, *Tongue of Flame: The Life of Lydia Maria Child (New York: Crowell, 1965); Jane and William Pease, Bound with Them in Chains: A Biographical History of the Antislavery Movement* (Westport, Conn.: Greenwood Press, 1972); Samuel Sillen, *Women Against Slavery* (New York: Masses and Mainstream, 1955); Alma Lutz, *Crusade for Freedom: Women in the Antislavery Movement* (Boston: Beacon Press, 1968).

9. Judith Wellman, " 'Are We Aliens Because We Are Women?' Female Abolitionists and Abolitionist Petitions in Upstate New York" (Paper presented to the National Archives Conference, Washington, D.C., April 1976); Wellman, "To the 'Fathers and Rulers of our Country': Abolitionist Petitions and Female Abolitionists in Paris, New York, 1835–1845" (Paper delivered at the Berkshire Conference

on Women's History, June 1976); Patricia Heard, " 'One Blood All Nations': Antislavery Petitions in Sandwich," and Ellen Langenheim Henle, " 'Forget Not the Matron': Sandwich Women and Antislavery in the Antebellum Years," *Fifty-Ninth Annual Excursion of the Sandwich Historical Society*, August 27, 1978; Gerda Lerner, "The Political Activity of Antislavery Women," in *The Majority Finds Its Past* (New York: Oxford University Press, 1980).

10. Birney quoted in James B. Stewart, *Holy Warriors: The Abolitionists and American Slavery* (New York: Hill and Wang, 1976), p. 81; Thomas Wentworth Higginson, *Cheerful Yesterdays* (New York: Arno Press[1899] 1968), p. 115; Goodell to *The Liberator*, February 20, 1836; Ward Family Papers, "Essay on Slavery," n.d., Box 22, Folder 2, American Antiquarian Society, Worcester, Massachusetts.

APPENDIX B

Notes on the Methods of this Study

The huge body of petitions in the United States National Archives is available to researchers. It is in Record Group 233 (House of Representatives) and Record Group 46 (Senate) of the Legislative Branch, Civil Archives Division.

The collection of antislavery petitions of the 19th to 38th Congresses was the starting point for the research. Memorials, petitions, and protests from citizens are noted in the *Journal* of each part of the national legislature. Their indexes take one to the appropriate pages on which are brief descriptions of the messages. For example, "Mr. Pomeroy presented a petition of citizens of Philadelphia and LeRay, New York, praying the total abolition of slavery throughout the country; which was referred to the Committee on the Judiciary." More specific directions to the locations of petitions are to be found in the inventories compiled by the Legislative Branch of the Archives. Finally, the petitions may be consulted only after receiving the written permission of the Clerk of the House of Representatives.

In each instance the petition under study was printed. A list of signatures followed the appeal or protest message. For example, the petition of Lynn citizens to the 24th Congress on March 21, 1836, contained a printed appeal for immediate emancipation in the District of Columbia of "upwards of six thousand of our fellow citizens." Two hundred and sixty-eight signers subscribed to the appeal. There are no other identifications on the petitions.

The task then became to link the names to several sources. Some of these were the 1850 federal manuscript census, the 1855 New York State manuscript and printed census, city directories, local tax assessors' lists, church records, membership lists of antislavery societies, mechanics' associations, temperance societies, workingmen's benefit societies (in this case the leadership of the Lynn society), factory payroll records, biographical compendia in local historical societies and libraries, and newspapers and antislavery journals. Local histories and the works of other historians were also consulted for any possible mention of names found in the petitions under study.

The volume of names made it necessary to limit the sample in order to make the project manageable. At first I created an alphabetical card file of legible names. In some of the cities I used more than one petition in order to arrive at a usable number. Utica, Lynn, and Fall River were such cities (see Tables B–1, B–2, and B–3). Duplication was eliminated and so were men with identical names. During the process of linking the remaining names, many were dropped from the sample because of ambiguity or uncertainty in the data. The result was a sample of from 20 to 50 percent of the original number of signers. For example, 677 men out of 1,624 signers on petitions of the 1830s became the operating sample of Utica, Rome, Schenectady, and Fall River. The same procedure was followed with the 1854 anti–Nebraska Act memorials for those cities. The cards in the file became a registry of all the discovered data about the signers.

In order to avoid becoming swamped by the numbers I later made a systematic sampling of Worcester, Springfield, and Lynn petitions by taking every second name from those lists. In some cities the selection had to be resumed after the first linkage was halted because it yielded so few operational names. As the data in this study indicate, I was left with small 1830s samples in Rome and Schenectady.

As the files grew to hundreds of cards, I turned to the computer for assistance. Computer scientists at the State University College at Potsdam, New York, where I was teaching, helped me to create a program and to begin the collection, description, and analysis of the data. Especially helpful, patient, and tolerant of this novice in their midst were Mr. Claude Lee LaBarre and Ms. Brenda Bergstrom. Mr. LeBarre was my shepherd through two years of the project.

With their advice and guidance I used the Statistical Package for the Social Sciences (SPSS) which was designed to facilitate such a project as mine. My design was not unlike modern social scientists' survey data analysis, even though mine did not come directly from interrogations of living persons. A code book was created with numerical values for forty-three variables. In the end, data in sufficiently usable numbers was discovered for only a few of these variables.

The printed 1830 and 1840 United States censuses provided population data and aggregates of age groups and birthplaces. Identification numbers for each of the men in the data bank came from the dwelling and household numbers of the manuscript censuses. The most available descriptive pieces of information in the censuses were: occupation, age, birthplace, and value of real property. However, local tax assessors' lists yielded more dependable real estate values than the census figures, which were the estimates of census takers or of the household heads in the survey. Personal property values came from city assessor lists. Church affiliations were discovered in church membership, baptism, marriage, and death records. Antislavery membership lists were found only for Lynn and Worcester in their respective local history societies and at the American Antiquarian Society in Worcester.

A variable became usable only when it encompassed a statistically significant body of petitioners. The problem may be appreciated by observing the tables for occupation, property assessments, church membership, and birthplace. Even some of these statistics may not be considered carved in granite. For example, church records were not available for all denominations in all of the cities. Tax records of the 1830s were absent in the New York towns except for Utica's 1835 listing; Springfield's 1854 records were not located.

A major lacuna is the large number of men missing from

1850 census listings for the cities in which they signed petitions. In addition the absence of city directories in several cities in the 1830s (Schenectady, Springfield and Worcester) and one in the 1850s (Ogdensburgh) proved frustrating. However, the earliest possible directory was used, as with the 1841 Schenectady and the 1845 Springfield and Worcester listings. The void suggests the great residential mobility in the antebellum Northeast.

There is some solace in knowing about high percentages of movement, but it fails to compensate for the sense of loss to scholarship of the hundreds who could not be identified. At best we may surmise that the missing men probably were the job and opportunity seekers, the uprooted and tramping artisans, laborers, farm laborers, immigrants from abroad, and the propertyless. This could be of great importance in characterizing the antislavery rank and file, but it must remain in the realm of speculation.

City directories were most valuable for their entries of occupations even though they were biased in favor of skilled tradesmen. Directories were found for the 1830s in Utica and Lynn; Schenectady, Springfield, and Worcester in the 1840s; and for all of the larger cities in the 1850s. No directories were found for New Hartford, Harvard, and Northborough. Occupational titles came from the 1850 census as well as from these city directories.

Even these two sources could not furnish foolproof job designations. A gap of from five to fourteen years between the date of a signature on a petition and the directory or census listing caused the loss of considerable numbers of men from our view. In Lynn, for example, an 1838 petitioner's occupation remained unknown unless his name appeared in the 1832 or 1841 directories or in the 1850 census. The latter was also used to corroborate some directory listings. I followed a procedure of reading back from 1850, based on an assumption that a man's occupation in 1850 probably was the same as it was in 1836–39 if he was also shown to have been thirty years or older in the 1850 census. Even though apprenticeship had been dying out in the face of early industrialization, the initiation into a trade and the world of work for wages often began at puberty. By the age of eighteen or nineteen, one could assume, a man was more or less established in a calling. To some extent this was also true of merchants and shopkeepers. Identification of occupation presented such a problem for the 1830s petitioners but not for the anti–Nebraska Act men. By the later period directory publishing appears to have become well established with the regular annual or biennial publication.

All of the collected data were run through two subprograms of SPSS. The first was FREQUENCIES, which provided the number and percentage of petitioners in each of the variables. The second was CROSS TABULATION, which provided two-dimensional comparisons of petitioners' characteristics. More sophisticated statistics were not attempted after an initial trial run. To have done so with such nominal data as a list of occupational titles or birthplaces would have been pointless and impractical. My decision to group age and property values forced me to use a hand calculator to find approximate mean age and mean property values of the petitioners. The computer would not have been able to produce a mean dollar value since it had been fed groups of values, such as $1,001 to $5,000. For this reason, and because much of the data of this type came from inconsistent sources, it was deemed wiser to avoid use of sophisticated statistical tests. The best that we could have hoped for would have been approximations.

The computer program was divided into three subfiles: STUDYNO 1 (New York and Massachusetts cities in the 1830s—Rome, Schenectady, and Utica, and Fall River, Springfield and Worcester); STUDYNO 2 (New York and Massachusetts cities in 1854–55—Lynn, New Hartford, and Ogdensburgh in addition to the cities in STUDYNO 1); STUDYNO 3 (Lynn in the 1830s—antislavery petitioners in this city on four dates between 1836 and 1839 plus 112 anti-abolitionists). STUDYNO 1 and STUDYNO 3 were combined to furnish two sets of tables for the 1830s: (1) antislavery petitioners, and (2) anti-abolitionists.

While a good profile of the male petitioners was emerging from the project, it was weakened by the failure to fully identify female petitioners. It was also lacking petitioners' political affiliations. As the work was nearing its completion I learned of the Lowell, Massachusetts, city directory's 1836 Female Supplement. I also learned of the Harvard and Northborough voters' lists. The first was through Thomas Dublin's doctoral dissertation on the mill women and the second came through the kind advice of Ronald Formisano.

Belatedly, these sources were linked to antislavery petitions in their respective towns. Sixteen of the twenty-one pages containing names of Lowell women in an 1836 petition were combed for those who were also in the Female Supplement and in the various companies' employee registers which Professor Dublin kindly sent to me. Professor Formisano took time from his duties at Clark University to meet me at the American Antiquarian Society and guide me to the Harvard and Northborough materials. These were linked to antislavery petitions which were among the large number from Worcester County. Neither the Lowell nor Harvard-Northborough studies were included in the computer program. Their relatively small numbers and my decision to limit the linkage to occupation influenced my course of action. I also wished to indulge a special interest—to make a case for factory operative antislavery activity.

Finally, the antislavery society membership lists of only two cities—Lynn and Worcester—presented some problems. The records of the group in the shoemaking city were at the Lynn Historical Society. The book of minutes contained the listing of men and women who were members between 1832 and 1839. This was a simple and clear record and easily linkable. The Worcester listing, however, presented a problem. It was a proposed constitution of the Worcester Anti-Slavery Society, undated but probably drawn up and signed about 1839–40. The signers resided both in the city of Worcester and in such surrounding towns as Shrewsbury and Millbury. Nonetheless, many of the signers were found in the 1845 city directory. I chose to use this list rather than the one drawn up earlier for the Worcester County southern division (which embraced the city). The names in it were linked to several other towns in the lower part of the county and proved unusable.

One important matter of omission requires explanation. Only

a handful of names on the petitions I studied turned out to be blacks, and I made no provision to differentiate the antislavery rank and file on race lines. Benjamin Quarles' admirable book *Black Abolitionists* (New York: Oxford University Press, 1969) provides a comprehensive study of the pioneering and continuous antislavery efforts of free blacks in northern towns and cities. Quarles did not present a systematic division of the black constituency on social class levels. But neither was he required to do so by the very nature of the evidence he found that pointed to entire black communities acting in concert. They were the earliest organizers of abolition societies and amassed petitions for state and national legislatures.

Table B-1
Size of Sample by Cities of Petitioners, 1854-55

City	Total No. Signers	No. in Sample	% of Total Sample
Ogdensburgh	307	184	10.8
Utica	755	361	21.0
New Hartford	188	119	6.9
Rome	360	88	5.1
Schenectady	514	291	16.9
Springfield	235	152	8.8
Worcester	138	108	6.3
Fall River	690	208	12.1
Lynn	870	209	12.2
Totals	4057	1720	100

Table B–2
Female Petitioners, 1830s; Selected Petitions

City	Petition Issue	Petition Date	No. of Signers	No. of Females Age 15–60+ yrs (approx.)	% of Females
Utica	Abolish slavery	3/21/1836	600	3500	17
Fall River	Abolish slavery in D. of C.	3/7/1836	376	1800	20.8
Lynn	D. of C. abolition	1/7/1839	912	2400	38
Lowell	D. of C. abolition	6/6/1836	1409	7000	20

Table B–3
Male Petitioners and Voters, 1830s; Sampled Petitions

City	Petition Issue	Petition Date	No. of Signers	No. of Voters *	No. of Males (15-60+ years)	Signers' % of Voters	Signers' % of Males
Fall River	DC Aboli-tion	2/18/39	195	893±	1130	41.0	32.0
	Texas Annex	3/12/38	363*				
	Gag Rule	2/18/39	149				
Lynn	DC Aboli-tion	3/21/36	268				
	Texas Annex	9/19/37	728*	1132	2300	64.0	31.6
	DC Abol.	1/3/38	555				
	DC Abol.	12/8/38	620				
	Gag Rule	3/12/38	860**			76.0	
Springfield	Gag Rule	2/14/38	538*	1386	2500	38.8	21.5
Worcester	DC Abol.	12/20/38	404*	894	1900	45.2	21.2
Rome	DC Abol.	1837	70	778	1600	8.9	4.3
Schenectady	DC Abol.	1838	119	1275	1740	9.0	6.8
Utica	DC Abol.	3/21/36	308*	1529	3600	20.0	8.5
	Texas Annex	9/19/37	110				
	DC Abol.	9/26/37	273				
	"Leaders"	1835-39	137				

* Largest petition from the city used in this study.

** Not sampled. Listed here to indicate largest male
   Petition from the cities studied here.

Index

About the Author

EDWARD MAGDOL (1918–1984) was an Honorary Fellow of the Department of History, University of Wisconsin-Madison, and Associate Professor Emeritus, Potsdam College of Arts and Science (State University of New York). He is the author of *Owen Lovejoy, Abolitionist in Congress* and *A Right to the Land, Essays on the Freedmen's Community;* and co-editor (with Jon L. Wakelyn) of *The Southern Common People: Studies in Nineteenth Century Social History.*